DESTROYING AMERICA

The Real Issues that Politicians Avoid

I0118598

DESTROYING AMERICA

The Real Issues that Politicians Avoid

Chris Florio

www.Destroying-America.com

ISBN 978-0-6151-7699-4

1. United States Government 2. Politics and corruption 3. Economics

Printed in the United States

My special thanks to my beloved Jodie for always being there,
Karlie for believing in me and the little buddy for telling me that I
had something worthwhile to say and to all of you who care enough
to read this

Contents

Introduction

DESTROYING AMERICA

The Real Issues that Politicians Avoid

Introduction - About me

So what makes you qualified to tell us about the issues in facing America and how to address them?

First because I really care about our country and unfortunately I have seen the same mistakes repeated by our government all of my life. I was brought up in a family to believe that anyone could be President, and that our votes counted for something, that this was the land of the free and the home of the brave and that this was the land of opportunity. I believe that I am uniquely qualified to write on behalf of what I would call the common man, I grew up in what I thought at the time was a middle class family but in looking back I would have to say that we were fairly poor living in a multi-ethnic, multi-racial neighborhood and I attended a pretty bad public school system. To spite getting in some trouble and attending many Yankee games I managed to get through school and get myself into college, the first one in my family to ever do so.

I struggled in college at first; I felt that most of my teachers really knew little more than I did about most of the subjects somehow I stumbled into reading and found that a book by an expert, such as a David Ogilvy on Advertising, on the subject of the class I was in was great supplemental material. I was constantly drawn into political and government books and amazed at the problems they illuminated, and I did an awful lot of reading my whole life. I was fortunate enough to have some really good teachers or I do not know if I would have stayed in school to this day I am grateful to them for making me want to learn.

I received my Bachelors degree while working full time, and experienced my first "recession" as I entered the job market for a better position with a $99 suit and a stack of resumes' in hand. While I did not land a "dream" job it was better money and definitely paying the bills I was bitten by the knowledge bug and decide to take a few MBA courses at night simply because I thought that it would look good on my resume, nothing more. A few years later I graduated my MBA program as Delta Mu Delta with honors.

I have lived on both coasts and travelled and stayed in most major metro areas, I have blue collar friends and white collar friends, I have experience in a variety of different cultures, I worked hard and got promoted, I worked harder and lost my job in the dot com implosion, I have seen good moments in people and bad. My observations are not from the ivory tower or Utopia of a college campus or from someone who never worked a day in there life, or who never dug a ditch, and I feel this puts me more in the common man category than hundreds of other so called experts. I also do not have an agenda, I am more rounded and balanced and I can see both sides of an issue, and I am not running for office, some of the things I say are going to anger the Republicans and some will anger the Democrats but no one is right 100% of the time, one thing I can say is that it is well past due that these topics come to light and are solved in a responsible manner with our elected officials.

Over the last 7-10 years I have had the good fortune of being able to do a lot of research while working on projects, the value in having the Internet is that you can learn the basics of a topic fairly quickly and never have to go to the library. There is a wealth of information out there and many people with great ideas, while I do not have all the answers and I never will but there is no shortage of intellectual talent in our great country and no problem that we can not solve if we work together. We first have to admit there is a problem. What I have seen is commonality in various works different people describing the same problem in various ways, various addictions, and common threads running through the social fabric but not connecting all the different pieces. This material will be presented as non partisan as possible. In some cases some of these subjects sometimes feel like we are preaching to the choir, but in order to intelligently consider a solution it is necessary to review what caused the problems and the background. Our elected officials are not learning from the previous mistakes part of that is because of the 4 year shelf life.

I have reached various conclusions on the topics presented; this is not based upon a conservative bias, or liberal bias, or a Democratic Party viewpoint or a Republican Party viewpoint none of that is important. No one in America should make up their mind based upon what Fox news thinks or the NY Times or what the party line is, this is a very dangerous trap we have fallen into. The only reason you should have an opinion or viewpoint on any topic is because you used your critical thinking skills to look at the facts, read both sides arguments and evaluated the issue based upon your experiences using your reasoning skills to form an opinion. And you considered the implications of a decision. Not because Ann Coulter said so or Hillary Clinton said so or some other expert said so. If you have not evaluated the facts you do not have enough information to agree or disagree with anyone.

Polls are not important as to what you think only what group you fall into on a subject because some number of people believes something does not mean they are correct. We do not need candidates that pander to polls we need candidates with convictions that will stick to those positions because they have examined the facts and made good decisions, not because of a poll. And the various buzzword labels of liberal, conservative, really stifle any kind of creative input as to resolution, nothing will stop an open exchange of ideas faster than name-calling. I am trying to do my part without having a TV show and outline a path to a solution in the hopes that this will stimulate debate and action.

Communication even between two people who are familiar with a topic and working closely together can be misunderstood and misconstrued, imagine throwing in numerous differing opinions, different cultures among many people. When discussing a political topic I feel it is important to clearly define what aspect of the issue and what it will solve rather resorting to general terms. All too often I have watched our elected official ramble on at length on some Sunday politics show only to say absolutely nothing, nothing of any substance. The Iraq conflict has actually made communication more difficult and even more important to clearly define what point you are speaking to, as politicians lambaste each other for your amusement over the slightest innocuous phrase. Until you either fall into the "with us" category or into the "terrorist" category there is no 3rd flavor here its all or nothing. If you carefully watch some of these shows you will see that what they do is no different than: Mr. Smith thank you for being on the show, now do like to beat you wife before or after dinner? This will not provide any basis or substance from which to create a solution, its just entertainment and it should not be confused with journalism.

For the most part I can tell you verbatim what the next candidate who will step up and run for office will say without knowing them, the position, or the state they are running in. It will be all the clichés that are normally touted. They will say: This is a time for a change and I am the candidate for change, I want to reduce government spending, I want to create more jobs, I will keep inflation down, we need to send someone to Washington to fight for right things, I am concerned with our children's future, when you elect me I will be a man of the people and I will go to work for you." What do you think? Is that about 90% accurate? But what does this mean? Well if you read it again it doesn't really say anything. What is a candidate for change? Change what? Your socks? Reduce spending by doing what? How are you creating more jobs? What kind of jobs? What concerns you about our children's future? It's a very nice clichéd paragraph but unfortunately it does not mean anything, he could think the right thing to do is raise taxes to 90% on everyone and that is the "right thing to do". We can not let elected officials get away with broad useless statements any longer, without the how and the why they are worthless comments a waste of everyone's time. Ask the question: How are you going to do it?

Our government is a very complex system and on the topics of controlling the national debt, balancing the budget and campaign finance reform while they are three separate topics they are highly interrelated. The solution must include all three subjects or it will never work, it will fail before it starts. This would be like taking cholesterol medication and having an all cheese and bacon diet you must address all three issues or you solve nothing. There are parts of our government that have simply become a system of legalized corruption they should be examined using the founding fathers as a guide, what would they do? An irony is that we are all paying for a government that is not working. In many cases our government is not working and we are getting the government that we deserve because we have been sheep in the process. Democracy in the current form is still only a 230 year old experiment based upon the premise of people knowing right from wrong and acting in the best interests of the people, this also means that based upon 51% of the vote that we all eat vanilla. The topics that follow are truly important to the future of our country you may agree with what I say, you may like part of what I say, you may hate what I say but the important thing will be that you cared enough to read it and form an opinion so you can tell your representative what they need to do.

The very greatness of our society has spoiled us and given us a touch of apathy from time to time where every problem facing America is somebody else's problem, let me tell you something if you pay taxes then these are your problems. I conclude the book with premise that as the most powerful industrialized nation with the greatest minds on the planet, that we can do as we have done before in mobilizing for World War 2 and bringing victory and again in the Apollo moon race to band together as a country to create a nationwide system of renewable energy in our country that makes the world green with envy as they are today with our technology. We need leaders in our country who inspire our greatness, who lead by aspiration and hope instead of by fear. This is our future and we can do it all we need is a leader with vision who is not afraid to stand up and start something that will not be easy, take our country back from special interests and free us from the dependence of oil. In our country it is time to be patriotic about something other than war.

DESTROYING AMERICA

Chapter 1 – What is Destroying America?

America has long been known as the land of the free and the home of the brave which it is. The Statue of Liberty proudly proclaims give us your tired your poor your huddled masses and we are known around the world as the beacon of hope and freedom, the land of opportunity. Many of us view America through rose colored glasses because it's special, because of our pride, because it's our home, but we are looking at an old nostalgic Rockwell picture not reality. But America is embarking into dark uncharted waters and government policy has strayed too far from what the forefathers envisioned and far off the path of common sense. And while there are numerous great things that America stands for, such as human rights, personal freedom, equality, free press, religion, and democracy there is a staggering and growing list of problems which this generation must face and prevail over.

Because of the way we allow Washington to run its day to day business we the people are the holders of a national debt nearing $10 trillion dollars. Our national debt has been accumulating long before World War II and while debt is a normal process of borrowing and using money the way in which our government uses debt is far from normal. As a percentage of our annual budget our payments on just the interest portion of the national debt is now over 20%, paying interest only never retires the principal, which is not a sound fiscal policy and secondly interest rates are at an artificial all-time low and when the rates do rise these payments will rise with them. Last year the payments made on the interest on the national debt amounted to $400 billion total, the actual amount owed was $550 billion but we stole $150 billion from Social Security payments to fund our debt. Without a balanced budget sooner or later some party will run us right into ground, if it is not to late already. This is not another prophet declaring the end is near and the "the sky is falling" this is very simple basic math, and one way or another will fall back on the taxpayer to carry this burden. Each month the Federal Reserve follows a process known as "surfing" to keep our economy alive, surfing is where the bank loans you more money to pay the interest on what they previously loaned you. Try this, call your bank and see if you can pay your MasterCard off with your Visa and next month, reverse it, pay Visa bill with your MasterCard, see how long you can play this game until it becomes a disaster. If you do it you are a fool, when the Government does this it is "fiscal policy", who's the fool? Everyone has left this problem for somebody else at $10 Trillion dollars and 20% of our daily budget the monster has grown large enough. It is becoming unmanageable based upon other looming economic realities.

The national debt stems from a simple yet very difficult problem, spending money, one of our countries addictions is spending money, my money, your money, everyone's money, money they don't have, imaginary money, fake money, printed money, any money it can even think about. A very simple and straight forward answer, there must be a balanced budget. Our government can no longer go about its daily affairs running a $2.5 Trillion dollar annual budget as if it were a spoiled child who blew his allowance on the movies and now wants a trip to toy store on your MasterCard. A little screw up from time to time is one thing, but this is normal policy, we have

$10 Trillion dollars unaccounted for. Our lawmakers never met a project they did not like, and as long as "it's just going on top of the pile", hey why not? A balanced budget restores accountability. No organization responsible for money, public, private or charity would be allowed to do what the government is doing. There should be no double standard for government the largest organization in the country should be and MUST be fiscally responsible. If you ran your business the way the government runs there's you would be out of business. The government should lead by example after all the government expects you fully obey, comply and follow all the laws of our country, when they can not balance a check book. A balanced budget insures the national debt will not increase and ends the runaway spending, corruption, graft, and greed. Throwing money at a problem does not fix the problem, finding a smart course of action to fix the problem and executing the plan solves the problem. I need only point to farm subsidies, the War on Poverty, the War on Drugs and our current education system to demonstrate that more money is not solving the problem; moreover each of these programs mentioned has become self perpetuating bureaucracy fully insolated from oversight and review.

As the baby boomers retire there will be more retirees moving to Social Security than ever in the history of our country this burden falls squarely upon the working class because there is no money in our Social Security fund we have been using it for day-to-day cash flow problems, however this bill is coming due. Numerous experts put this expense in the $30 to $60 to $120 trillion dollar range this dwarfs our national debt in terms of total expense. This is a staggering amount of money. Unfortunately there is no money put aside for Social Security and Medicare and as the demographics shift and there are less workers to support each retired person obviously the mathematics are not going to work. Never before have the finances of our country being tested in this manner with the massive shift of the workforce no longer producing income but expecting the social safety net and benefits promised to them under Social Security, which they have paid into and fully funded. If these current economic conditions persist these trends will undoubtedly put an economic strain on the entire workforce. This is a concern because our economy is not growing in double digits, barely single digits at times, from looking at the real CPI data one could make the argument that it is not growing at all. When you add the national debt, decrease in workforce, and increase in Social Security and Medicare spending all at the same time, you do not need to be Albert Einstein to see that there is a major challenge ahead.

We always envision ourselves as the greatest nation in the world so it is hard to fathom that other nations are far ahead of us in health care. Currently there are 50 million Americans who do not have health care in a country of 300 million. This means 1 out of 6 people in our country have no health benefits. This is not a problem limited to uninsured people in a vacuum because these uninsured citizens add to the cost of those who are insured so this is a real problem in real dollars. The amount of uncovered people also slips by government experts when they tout productivity, CPI gains, low-inflation and a strong economy, the fact that there are 50 million Americans that do not have health care obviously raises the costs of health care to everyone else. Whether it is called socialized medicine or universal health care or the magical health system the framework for such a system is already in place so that most of the system can still function it would just be a different payer it wouldn't look much different from an HMO or PPO plan. I find it appalling that in the greatest nation almost 20% of our citizenry has no health coverage and other countries have far better healthcare systems than we do, and there is no reason for this to continue there are a number of things that can be done but unfortunately Congress will need to act in order to make this happen. Incidentally the members of Congress have a fantastic healthcare benefits plan that we pay for, but no one calls it socialized medicine.

Another difficult fact that we must come to terms with is the fact that our country is falling far behind in education. America is currently ranked in the bottom quartile of the top 25 industrialized nations in education, there is no reason for this and it must change. When I read this statistic at first I could not believe it, I think we all have a certain pride about our country, but we can not afford to let our pride blind us. Our country was not #1 or in the top ten it was not even in the top half of all countries. We currently have the least amount of students at college level science and mathematics, and our students can't even place in the 50 percentile versus German and Belgian and European schools in the same grade level. All rhetoric aside our children are our future and if this is the greatest country in the world and we can't be in the top five there is a problem, and in order for us to keep an advantage we must change what we're doing and make it work. We spend hundreds of millions of dollars on education and the test scores and comparisons to other countries show a continuous decline of American education this is an unsettling fact based upon the outlays tendered for education system. Without producing the best students and most qualified students in needed fields of science and mathematics the United States will fall further behind as other countries now begin to emerge in the global talent pool, we cannot afford to let this happen. And while everyone is touting that no child is left behind not only are they left behind but the top ones are only mediocre versus their peers, a slogan is not a plan.

In 2006 America spent $522 billion on defense. Which did not include expenditures for the war in Iraq, which at the time of writing this was approaching $1 trillion (CBO Estimate of $2.4 Trillion and a higher estimate of $3.5 Trillion by 2019). In 2007 America will spend close to $625 billion on defense. America is not involved in any major conflict other than Iraq, yet it spends money as if it was fighting World War III and WW4 and WW5 all at the same time. Case in point from 1990 and before through 2007 America spent more than half of the entire outlays for all military expenditures in the whole world, let me reiterate 50% of all military spending of the entire world total is spent by America, we have 6% of the worlds population but spend 50% of all the money spent on weapons in the world. This we are "Sparta" mindset is unacceptable in our modern times the cold war is over we would expect this behavior to be something done by only a war mongering insanely military nation. If any other country was spending this amount of money on its military we would call them a dangerous nation, but we are the ones doing this. We are not fighting the whole world and need to stop spending money as if we were involved in several world wars it has no tangible benefit nor will it solve any of our real problems. Defense and security are important components of our annual budget but the spending levels are far too high in relation to other budget items, for example the department Defense outlays is higher than the total outlays of the other 18 departments of our government combined. We can not afford this constant preparation for Armageddon without dire financial consequences.

Campaign Finance

In 2006 over $3.5 Billion was spent lobbying Congress. These are funds that we are aware of it is easy to theorize that it least this amount was spent for influence without being reported. This is PAC money, corporate interests' money and special interests; with this amount of money being spent it is easy to see who has influence in Congress and the Senate. And when issues are taken into consideration and decided just to the interests are satisfied. This is the semitransparent side of American politics what exactly does a $1 million campaign contribution mean? What did that buy you? We would like to think that everyone's vote and voice or equal but clearly as representatives live and die by campaign contributions one can see just how important these special interests become. And if the elected representatives are not serving the people then they are not doing their job if they are not doing what they are chartered to do by the Constitution of the United States. Our legislative body then becomes a tool of the corporations and extension of the donations which are received in any other country this would be called a bribe. When Congress now decides matters based upon campaign contributions we are no longer living in a democracy, and we cannot be deluded into thinking that we all are. Finance Reform gets rid of Gucci gulch (lobbyists) and gets the Congress back to representing the people and not the lobbyists, what a concept. We must also make the elected officials accountable and responsible for their actions spending whatever they want and throwing the debt on top of the pile is no longer an acceptable practice.

Size of Government

I will go through the numbers in detail in a later chapter, but it appears that either directly or indirectly that the government of the United States is responsible for almost 44% of the workforce. We must embrace economic basics here if the government is overhead every additional person working in government places a burden on us all. While there must always be an administrative overhead and a governmental body we must examine what percentage is of marginal utility adds in a classic Keynesian model. Because obviously for every additional person there is additional overhead for more overhead the higher the tax rate the more money you will take from each working individual, this point is rudimentary but as the size of government has increased the burden placed on each worker has increased thusly. We don't need more government we don't need more taxes, we need more private sector jobs, we need less people in Government jobs to do more with less money and every additional person over a say 10%-15% administrative overhead must be justified. By reducing the size of government we will reduce the burden on each worker and that tax rates that are applied to each worker. As Communism has proved the government is not the most appropriate arbiter of resources this affects real jobs in the real world and allocation of resources. We have strayed off Laissez-faire, "Adam Smith" invisible hand economy as our founding fathers have warned would create problems and we are facing these problems and costs everyday. Instead of increasing the size of government we need to look at a Zero Base Budgeting and eliminate programs which have just become self perpetuating institutions.

Tax Code

Our current tax code is over 10,000 pages and replete with loopholes that you could drive an aircraft carrier through. As most people know a normal family of four 1040 tax return was brought to 50 independent CPAs and came back with 50 different returns with 50 different amounts of taxes owed. There is no room in our country for something with so many gray areas that there can be 50 different answers that are correct. Ronald Reagan tried to simplify the tax code he succeeded to some extent. As of 2005 there have been 14,000 amendments to the tax code. The code as it exists is nothing but loopholes for special interests and people that have paid for considerations for certain items. The smartest thing that we can do would be to scrap the code entirely and go with a flat tax eliminating all the bull shit, complex provisions special rules and governmental nauseam. How such a gray area document could become law is simply a matter of contributions from special interests we certainly do not need to endorse this policy to continue to be how we tax people, it is an outdated overly complex bag of shit. The entire concept of taxation without representation that our forefathers fought so proudly against seems to be entirely lost to our people. Taxation has found its way into every facet of our lives, you wake up in the morning and turn on the lights and the electricity that you use is taxed, turn on the shower, the water you used is taxed, get in your car, you paid sales tax on the car, and registration on the car is a form of a tax, fill your car with gas, and the gas is taxed, federal, state and local, drive to work and work the first 4 hours to pay to pay Federal, State, Local, Social Security, Medicare, FICA, Disability, AMT, and any other tax, you go to lunch and pay a sales tax on your sandwich. Use your cell phone it is taxed, go home after work, make sure you pay your real estate taxes, wake up tomorrow and start again. Moreover most of the examples above are regressive taxes because you are paying an additional tax with after tax dollars, the government gets the first cut of your money and then nickels and dimes you on every necessity of life.

Work Force

We are a versatile and talented people; we have gone from a population of 98% of farmers in Jefferson's time to where we are today. Over the years a great number of manufacturing and higher paying jobs have been outsourced overseas, Canada, Mexico for numerous reasons. Wages are an obvious problem in our part of the expense to the company but there are underlying factors in the cost of employment in the United States such as insurance, healthcare, the State burden rate which is why these jobs have moved out of our country. Unless we address unfair shifts in costs to employers and the evolution of the global workforce we will be caught far behind. There is a much needed recharging and retooling of our workforce based upon changes in the workplace and computerization. If we do not retrain our workforce they will be unable to fill the jobs of the 21st century, this has already been proven because of the recent trends in outsourcing these types of positions to India and other countries. If we do not remain competitive in this area more jobs will leave the country this is a fact. As more positions are shifted to a global workforce and away from United States this will impact our workforce and economy. Since we are now predicated on a service-based economy for more positions we lose in this vertical the more of an impact it will have on our economy. It was 1991 when service jobs outpaced manufacturing for the first time, now paper shuffling, administration, and intangible goods make up the majority of our economy. Look at all the mortgages in 2001-2005 a mortgage is a service, nothing was built or created simply paper moved around, the banks made money you did not. Nothing was created or exported. The idea of 25-30 years at the same company, the pension and the gold watch have gone the way of Santa Claus and our workforce needs to adapt or die.

End of Pork Spending and Spending in General
We spent over $31 Billion dollars on Pork projects in 2006, this is simply something we can no longer afford to do. We need to look to the future and

work towards a common vision. Not support random project of dubious value. The entire concept of "bringing home the bacon" needs to end, because the chairman of the Highway funding committee was from Alaska the LEAST populous state he was getting the largest cut of the highway spending pie. While that's a good cigar story and an atta'boy at a cocktail party with his financiers and benefactors, it does not help our country it does not benefit Joe Citizen. And this needs to be part of the changes listed above or none of them will have any profound effect. Because the current process of spending any amount of money on anything you want while being influenced by large corporate donations has gotten us to where we are, so we have proven that the current political process is broken and in desperate need of an overhaul. Further institute process change such as, if you are on the highway committee you can not get any highway funds for your state, make it as unbiased and objective as possible. This puts an end to a $700 million bridge in Alaska because it's "my" budget, its not "your" budget its our countries money and our future not your personal piggybank. Also institute a simple Non-Compete clause for all representatives, if you are a member of the banking process reform committee you can NOT quit on a Friday and go to work for the enemy and lobby for the banks on Monday, includes staff, appointees etc. Enough of the good'ol boy network it gets us no where and costs us billions of dollars. Lastly we need the Death penalty for members of government caught with their hand in the cash register. This is no different than treason which is punishable by death. There was a Congressman in Louisiana with $90,000 in his freezer and one in San Diego driving a Bentley, jail time is one thing but if these people knew they could be put to death for this type of behavior it would change their status quo mindset. These are our elected representatives and they should be held to a higher standard.

Over 5% of our population is incarcerated costing a national average of $40,000 per inmate per year. In the past 10 years the number of drug related convictions was close to 70-75% of the inmate population. What we need is drug treatment programs that work not inmate housing, we have more people percentage wise to our total population in jail in our free country than Russia did at the height of Communism. This needs to change. Remember prohibition was less than 100 years ago and alcohol was the devils brew.

Immigration is another issue that needs to be addressed and a comprehensive detailed solution must be implemented. These are complex issues that can not be answered in a 7 second sound bite on CNN, there are few yes/no answers and various ranges of outcomes that require intelligent discussion. For this reason politicians avoid them a complex question that could make me look bad depending on who is watching, no comment. That's why Congress investigates Steroids in Baseball, and passes Child pornography laws they like the meaningless inquiries and the slam dunk stick to the sex offender type issues, nice and easy. Leave the tough problems to the next generation. Unfortunately that is us.

The Tent Stakes of Stupidity.

I will detail in chapter 10 the tent stakes of stupidity. These are by and large the "big issues" that divide the parties. Capital Punishment, Abortion, Gun Control, Pledge of Allegiance (the word "God" being included), teaching evolution in schools (Darwin) etc, with Gay Marriage and Medically Assisted suicide poking their head in from time to time and as of late "intelligent Design". But what they really are is nothing. These are nothing more than "weapons of" "mass distractions" to coin a phrase from Robin

Williams in his movie Man of the Year were he played a pundit running for President. Regardless of whatever the outcome or standing of any politician on anyone of these issues there is a 95% chance it will never affect you or anyone that you know. Voting for a candidate because he is for Capital punishment or for Gun control is not a reason to elect someone this is all a sideshow for the 5% who care about that issue and an insult to the rest of us. Is the candidate for reducing the size of government? Balancing the budget? Reducing foreign aid? These are important issues not scenery, vote on important issues not freak show politics. Polarize and marginalize as many voters as you can and avoid all the hard topics.

Vision and Leadership

We have been preoccupied with the conflict in Iraq for a number of years, and we need to move forward again. Thirteen colonies added the Louisiana Purchase, and then added California; we connected our country with new technology called railroads, then telegraphs. This was followed by the rural electrification act, bringing electricity throughout our country. Eisenhower saw the need for an Interstate highway system, John Kennedy challenged us to land on the moon and we did. None of these achievements were easy, nor did they happen overnight. Because provided that there is vision and leadership there is no lack of skill, ingenuity and determination like that of the American will to "get it done". We need to get our country off the dependence of foreign oil with a finite and real time limit. We have the technology and the resources and we can beat the addiction. It is vital to our national security and our entire economy that we not be dependent to hostile unstable regions for our supply of oil. Wind, Solar, Tidal and Geothermal energy is our future we need to embrace it and invest in it. And begin using it immediately. As Asia's consumer base picks up the demand for oil will push the price up constantly and there are 3 Billion consumers about to be born in the China, India, and the Pakistan region alone, this will adversely impact world supply. There is more on this in Chapter 14.

America 2.0

Why a Band aid will not work. In order for our country to move forward it must be fiscally sound as well as have good management. The government should not be exempt from something you learn on the first day of accounting 101, balance the books. This is no different than running your household finances or running a company except that it is obviously a lot larger. Since this is public money they should be held to a higher standard not a lower one. If you run a small business and have a budget and you constantly fall short of cash you are not running your business very well, as a matter of fact you would be out of business if you continued doing that, so why do we let Washington run our country this way? If on a personal level you maxed out a different credit card every month sooner or later you would have serious financial problems this is no different for our government. This is why we must have a balanced budget, a balanced budget restores responsibility to our elected officials, it does not leave a legacy of debt to our great grand children. In 2006 The US Government spent $2.5 Trillion dollars, ($1.5B per hour) sorry guys $2.5 Trillion dollars is enough, Washington you are going to have to scrimp by.

A balanced budget is fiscal responsibility. A balanced budget insures that our debt levels are not constantly rising, because rising debt levels cut into our daily operating budget and take money away from other necessary budget items. Very simply if we continue to increase our debt that money will have to come from somewhere, and somewhere is you and me, in the form of taxes. We must stop looking at government through the rose colored glasses of a child, any bill they incur, is a bill that WE incur, whether it be a $400 hammer or the Space Shuttle it gets paid by us and passed on to our children, there is no free lunch ever, anywhere. Managing and reducing our debt over time is a fiscally responsible and necessary process, paying interest only was short term thinking because politicians only think short term, 4 years actually. Future outlays on T-Bills should have triggers and debt retirement mechanisms, and while it will cost more in the short run, the debt will be retired in 25-30 years, not be a runaway MasterCard on steroids. With all the geniuses on Wall Street there is no shortage of ideas of how to do something like this correctly. But no one in Government plans 30 years out they only worry about tomorrow and getting re-elected and if this is the case then we don't need them.

Understanding how we got to where we are is equally important because we do not wind up back here ever again. Every industry has lobbyists' and there own business and special interests, this is a natural outcropping, however when an industries agendas become law it is no longer natural, it is a paid process. The companies pay for influence and they get it, whatever amount of spending the government does because of special interests we will never know. But one thing we can be sure of is the $3.5 Billion dollars that we know about in "campaign" contributions makes our elected officials answer to the corporations and not us, in effect bypassing democracy. Since there is an unbalanced budget any project is possible since the "I don't have to pay for it" mentality pervades the status quo. Hence if we leave the current system in place it will only be a matter of time before it returns to its former self. If your child is writing on the wall with crayons after you scold them you do not leave the box of Crayola's sitting there do you? Having the politicians represent you instead of the special interests is their intended purpose and will go a long way in restoring our democracy and faith in government.

"We the People". In a way we can not lay the blame entirely on our elected officials what politician wants to say that the things you are asking me for will cost you money? Who wants to tell the people whom you are begging for their vote, that this will raise your taxes? Who doesn't want "free" money? No one. We all want free money, but there isn't any and there is no tooth fairy either. Our politicians spent all the money in the world and just threw the debt on top of the pile so they did not have to deliver bad news to us their constituents. So we are partly to blame. But we are not children anymore. While I did not sign up for this job let me deliver the bad news that has been in front of your eyes for the last 30 years, the current cost to us is 20% of our annual budget in debt payments and a $10 Trillion dollar debt. So this was never free money and the interest alone on all this "free" money is costing us $550 Billion per year. How does this really impact me? This means the taxes you pay could be 20% less. We have to stop behaving like children who do not want bad news and act like shareholders in a company or in this case a democracy. The current mindset of electing officials to make decisions for us so that we do not have to think has got us through the first 200 years, but seems dangerously outdated. The corruption, debt and broken processes that Washington has left behind are a testament to the need for an overhaul not only to our system but to our way of thinking.

By decreasing the size of government we lower the burden laid on each working individual, period. This is common sense not rocket science if there are 10 million government employees and we reduce it by 1 million employees that is 10% less. Each additional person, missile, bridge, and aircraft carrier puts a burden on all of us. We do not live in an age of rapid expansion those days are long behind us. When the economy expands rapidly there is the ability to service more debt more easily but as we mature as a nation our economy is less responsive and we fight a constant battle between inflation and recession, which I will discuss in a later chapter. Over the last 30 years wile there have been rampant advances in automation and computerization public employees have increased fivefold while the population has grown a scant 10% over the same period per decade so there is no correlation whatsoever as to why so many public sector jobs are needed. Most public sector jobs add nothing to the economy and are simply regulatory bodies, wonderful organizations such as the DMV, and the IRS quickly come to mind. These institutions entrench themselves in regulation and a complex mix of procedures and administrivia, there is no competition for what these bodies do and the service rendered is usually of the lowest quality possible. This is exactly what it happening in our schools right now and why they are failing, I will discuss this in a later chapter. If you simplify the tax code you eliminate all the people hiding behind the complex procedures and interpretations and hopefully put them into productive private sector jobs generating tax revenue instead of being a leech attached to the body. A certain amount of these jobs or gatekeepers will always be necessary but 9,000 pages of tax code insure that it can not ever be minimized. Add this complexity to 18 Federal government departments, each with their own sub departments and sub committees, then apply it across 50 State governments, county and local municipalities and any sense of progress quickly evaporates.

There will always be a need for traffic cops, and the tax collector. But the current economic model is that we increase last years budget by X% and while this may make sense it eliminates looking objectively at the problem and asking: do we need less? Not more. Which is why a tax never goes down or goes away, including the 1898 Federal Excise tax on phone service which was instituted to pay for the Spanish American war, which ended 107 years ago. In the private sector your ass is on the line everyday, there is no more 25 year gold watch mindset, your company can be bought, sold, bankrupt, merged, downsized, right-sized, outsourced, or eliminated on any given day. This never happens in the public sector, where more staff means "better service", where bigger budgets and more staff mean power and being in the private sector means taxpayer money not company money. Each dollar spent in the public sector is a dollar taken away from the private sector, there is only one pie that we all share from. Government positions are a necessary part of our society but not the amount that we have currently, nor can we sustain the growth of this sector.

Social Security. Various writers and economists have discussed the national debt doomsday clock and the unbalanced budget so what makes this not just another the sky-is-falling issue? Other extremely astute and intelligent economists and mathematicians have warned us before, these experts have not taken into consideration just how low the Federal reserve rate has been over the last 10 years, 7-10% interest rates were considered somewhat "normal" since the dot com bubble burst we have been at historical and artificial all-time lows, this keep the interest payments much lower, but causes other economic .problems. The Federal funds rate was under 2% for over 2 years, and under well under 3% for all 3 years (2002-2005) including a 1% range for a prolonged period. So these experts are right if you adjust the timeline. Compound Interest only goes up. With the baby boomers retiring and service jobs increasing while manufacturing jobs are disappearing the United States is going to traverse one of the largest demographic changes in its history, one with severe economic impact. Estimates say there will be 2.4 to 3.5 working people supporting 1 Social Security retiree, a very different calculation than 5-1 and 10-1 currently. Between Social Security and of course it will be gradual, 1% here, 2% there and over time they will take whatever they need from you. How do I know this? There is no where else to get it from.

This is why how much overhead and how many employees and current budgets in government are relevant. This Boomer Social Security issue is going to test our economy like no other event in our lifetime, and while it is important it is only part of what needs to be addressed within our government to restore accountability and responsibility to our democracy. With a current workforce of 140 Million and almost 70 million people due to retire by 2030 this will mean a great deal of changes are coming. We no longer have the luxury of passing the problem onto the next generation; we are the "next generation". Balancing our budget, controlling spending and solving our other financial problems, while reducing total overhead and the size of government will go a long way in resolving the Social Security issue.

DESTROYING AMERICA

Chapter 2 – Our Pile of Debt

Our first addiction: money. Our national debt currently approaching $10 Trillion dollars was created and increases every day because of the fiscal mismanagement and lack of accountability for spending taxpayer money by our elected officials. But make no mistake while we elected these officials and they created this problem, we are the holders of this bill and regardless of who's in office we ultimately are paying for it, will continue to pay for it, and will hand this down to our great-great grandchildren. It now accounts for 20c of every dollar the government spends. Debt when used properly is a useful financial tool for companies and organizations who use it responsibly however the private sector could never get away with using debt in the manner that the US government does. I will put forth a common sense argument regarding our national debt problem; there are no doubt numerous other points of view on the subject. I will detail to you why common sense is needed and the current course is criminal. Unfortunately most of the people with these "expert" opinions that a huge debt is good have a biased vested interest in keeping things the way they are. They either benefit from the continuance of status quo, such as the banking industry, or base perceptions upon other either largely miscalculated government statistics or percentage of GDP, but never allow for in the maturity or economy or factor and other real world variables, or worse are simply rendering an opinion from the Ivory towers of Academia that holds no water in the real world.

And to the average Joe or layman that says why do I care? You should care because the government takes their cut out of your paycheck before you see it, but then they are not done, it doesn't stop there. Even after taking their cut of taxes everything you do is taxed on your after-tax earnings. The debt is the difference between what is collected by the IRS and what is spent by the government. If we force the government to pass a balanced budget amendment it could no longer play this game in perpetuity. Based on the amount of interest being paid to service the national debt the average Joe could have 20% lower taxes, so that would be 20% of your taxes back in your pocket. The debt has been growing steadily and has past the stage of critical mass and when the government needs to increase their payments on the interest they will raise your taxes and take the money from you. Picture it this way right now .20c of every dollar the government gets its hands on disappears instantly, evaporates into thin air do you think that amount could go down? It will never go down or even level off unless we balance the budget.

So what started me on this, I took a good look around the country and said to myself well $10 trillion dollars what did we get? Are we safe? Is Social Security overflowing with surplus? Lots of money for medicare? Do we have the best health care of any industrialized nation? Are we investing in our future? Are our streets paved with gold? Do we have the best school system in the world? Did we eradicate poverty? Are we free from the dependence on foreign oil? Sadly, no, we have none of these things not a single one. None, ZERO. $10 Trillion dollars in the hole and we did not even get a free sandwich. Which begs the question with the government spending $2.5 trillion per year, Social Security bankrupt, $10 trillion in debt, where is this money going ? and with these results why in hell would we want to spend more in the same manner. These are the results of the current process which got us to our current state so we don't need to repeat or continue this process as there is more than ample hard evidence that it doesn't work and will continue to give us more of the same. To spend another $2.5 trillion next year and the year after that and still have 50 million Americans without health insurance, no money in Social Security no money in Medicare and a failing education system makes absolutely no sense whatsoever. So why do we continue to do it?

Because the budget for the federal government was $2.5 trillion last year 2006 that doesn't mean that we need to increase it next year that is another status quo fallacy that permeates government. Every year the machine gets bigger more complex takes on more moving parts and becomes impossible to dismantle; soon it is in self perpetuation another untouchable worthless bureaucracy. But it doesn't have to be this way it is unfortunate that we have to be the generation that realize that the party is over but the sooner we get on with the inevitable the better off our country will be. Just as you must abide by economic fundamentals to run your household corporations most abide by the rules of generally accepted accounting principles (GAAP) the federal government must balance their budget. This is the first and critical step in fiscal responsibility this restores the premise of common sense for the greater good and eliminates the ivory tower thinking of spending yourself out of a recession. Balancing the budget can mean lowering your taxes it also means giving up a $700 million bridge to nowhere, this is not necessarily a bad thing.

One of the common arguments for heavy government spending and debt creation is based upon the percentage of debt to the country's GDP or gross domestic product, because that makes it look tiny. The GDP of a country is defined as the total market value of all final goods and services produced within a country in a given period. The government's statisticians would argue that as long as the debt burden is correlated as a certain percentage of GDP that even though $10 trillion dollars seems like a lot of money you must compare it to the $13.5 trillion GDP. This is fine in the imaginary world of government mathematics and to a certain extent it's true but the main reason the scholars lean on this argument is because the national debt has spiraled out of control and passed any other factual setting that they could use as a point of reference. It is so large that there is nothing else the experts can compare it to. This also does not take into consideration that since the payments are based upon interest rates one year the payments are perfectly in line with all experts expectations, but what happens when the interest rate doubles? Or triples? Their fancy math goes out the fricking window because it's based on bullshit and its inconvenient to consider reality. Besides that GDP is a cooked number to begin with, because no matter what really is going on in the economy the government is going to show the world that there is X% percent of new growth in our economy, and regardless of the circumstances the government will find it, even if it's not there. Has there ever been a presidential administration that hasn't put the spin on "job growth", "trending", "turning around", "no inflation" are you better off today than you were four years ago? Spin of any bad data point as turning around and any good news as great, any number you don't like is "changing" or forecasted any number you do like is "very positive". Well here's where it gets even more convoluted the government's total spend annual $2.5 trillion is the major portion of the $13.5 trillion GDP total, so all the government needs to do to show growth or a higher GDP is spend more money that they don't have, that's right run up the national debt and show that GDP is solid and growing! Going deeper and deeper into hock to show a strong economy! So to rely on one abstract number as a factor for another abstract number and that are both manipulated will lead to an answer, albeit probably an incorrect one.

The other commonly known scholarly argument maintains that for a vibrant economy the government should maintain a higher debt level because it will be offset by the corresponding growth of the economy. Again another argument that on the surface rings true but once you look underneath the skin at what is really going on has little relevance. This premise is based upon a rapidly growing economy and even with the best numbers from the CPI and GDP we are treading about 1% growth not exactly what anyone would consider runaway growth. What you must understand is that with the current fiscal policy none of this debt is ever retired so any amount added to it becomes a payment in perpetuity, and never getting paid off and never lowering the principal for the end of time. So while there is a comfortable range as a percentage of your annual budget as we increase now to 20%, 21%, 22% these rates as a part of the whole budget will never decrease because the loan principle never gets paid off, who the hell would design a system this way? Who would paint themselves into a corner everyday? Another point to consider is that this is compound interest and because of the dot-com stock market meltdown coupled with the events of 9/11 this led to the Federal Reserve Bank lowering the federal funds rate to a 40 year low and maintaining them under 4% for a prolonged period of time. As interest rates rise so will our payments on the national debt and that $400 billion could easily double or triple which would make it half of our annual budget not 20% as it is today. And by the way it's really $550 billion dollars but they steal $150 billion from Social Security so the net is only $400 billion, but now the boomers or retiring.

The banking industry loves the government debt. You first must have a primer on the Federal Reserve Bank so let me explain the process and you will see why, the process does include some magical steps that you may not be aware of. So pay attention or you might miss it. The government has no money, no petty cash, no savings, nothing, so for anything the government needs to do it puts together basically a budget acquisition and authorizes the Federal Reserve Bank, to go to auction and sell Treasury Notes for the amount requested. By the way the Federal Reserve Bank is NOT part of the US government it is a private bank, so if you would ask why the government would go to a private institution to ask for money to operate you are too far ahead of me, hang on. The Fed sells the treasury bonds and puts the proceeds on deposit at the Federal Reserve Bank, and issues the government a credit from the proceeds from the auction, less the federal reserves fees, POOF, viola money is created out of thin air. (This was the magic part) The government then takes the credit and spends it as fast as they can, of course the first item paid is the interest on the debt, so the more the Fed loans the government the more it gets paid. Pretty nice arrangement! Guaranteed payments. And because of the amount of money constantly needed by the government no commercial bank could possibly compete. And the first cut of the money goes right back to the Fed, currently 20%, and the fed has no competitors. By the way the Federal Reserve was created by 10 Wall St bankers including J.P. Morgan and Paul Warburg in 1913 and passed into law by a bunch of very crooked politicians. It was passed in the middle of the night in the empty halls of Congress on December 23, 1913, with barely enough people present to hold a vote.

We have created a Fiat economy through the use of the Federal Reserve System, all the currency in the system is simply backed by the full faith and credit of the United States Government, whatever that means. The United States went off the gold standard in 1974 after the oil embargo crises of that period; our currency is not tied to gold reserves, which is good and bad. So one may ask: well this is the way things are so we have no choice but to deal with it? But this is not true, our government operated long before the creation of a central bank, a central bank is an idea we borrowed from communism. For 130 years the government ran without a federal reserve and with creating a fiat system. (and a first central bank which failed) In the 1860s President Abraham Lincoln instituted a Greenback system to stabilize a civil war torn economy, and this was one of the most stable economic periods in US history. The US Federal Reserve System makes the banking cartel very rich and you get to pay for it.

As if that wasn't a sweet enough deal but that's not all, you see the money deposited in the Federal reserve bank gets distributed to the 14 regional member banks and because of fractional reserve banking each bank can then loan out 10-40 times what ever is deposited, the process repeats downstream to smaller banks. All this money is "created" and 20 times the deposits can be loaned out so the banks love the Federal Reserve Banking system. You must forget the Frank Capra vision of banking from "It's a Wonderful Life" when Jimmy Stewart was trying to save his small town family bank by pleading: "Tom your deposit was loaned to Bob for his new roof", "Mary your deposit went for Bill's heart operation" etc. This might have been banking 50 years ago but not anymore. If a bank has $1 Million on deposit they can loan up to about $20 million dollars out maybe more, and how do banks make money? Banks get paid by taking the difference between what they collect for interest on loans less the interest they pay the depositors. So in this case they will pay out $50,000 (5%) for the $1 Million in deposits and collect (8%) $1.6 million dollars + fees for the loans, on the $20 Million that they loaned out, $20 Million which they do not have. So it's not a bad deal for the bank. None of this actually helps you or me. If you could loan out 20 times the money you had then you could make money to, but you would be arrested for fraud. The banks will also write off the bad loans and uncollected amounts of the money they loaned out but never had to begin with, they also get to seize and confiscate the property from the people they made the loan to.

But there are other issues caused by a United States funds its debt at the Treasury auctions we put a heavy demand on the world economy which we pay for in other ways. Most of our allies are no longer primary sources of funding as a matter of fact Communist China is now the largest buyer of our treasury notes we are reliant on a "third world" country to keep our economy moving. China has amassed over $1 trillion of the United States debt. Please note that while it may be good for the United States to find a buyer for these investment instruments it may not be in the best interests of the global economy meaning our appetite for inflow of cash in the world market is quite sizable, and while there is stability in the treasury bills for these kinds of outlays in cash most investors want a higher return. It will be difficult to compete with other investments that may make 10%, 20%, 50%, 100% versus the return of the T-bill. So in our avarice to run our country may be taking money away from the next IBM or similar enterprise getting funding. And while the CPI and other government math will show that there is no inflation any first-year economist will tell you that with this level of sales of T-bills that we are certainly devaluing our currency, so whether you want to say the prices are rising or the money is worth less the result will be the same. So many US Dollars in circulation makes them more and more a commodity.

So if you were the government and you wanted to buy a nice new $1,500 TV for the new apartment that you are moving in to, you would request it as a budget item, the Fed would have an auction and the proceeds would be deposited in the bank. You would then purchase the $1,500 TV. Every month the government would pay $50 for the TV. So after 30 months the government has paid $1500 for the TV set commerce what do you think they still owe? Well remember this as interest only so at the end of 30 months of $50 payments the government still owes $1500 on TV, another 30 months go by another $1500 in payments and we still owe $1500 for the TV. We will never pay it off, it will more than likely wind up in a dumpster and we still be paying for it because this is the method that the government uses for fiscal policy. This may seem a silly example but this is a simply an insane process, this is what our government does every day that's why there's a $10 trillion bill with your name on.

Many people may think "Okay so this is a debt we owe ourselves so what's the big deal if we just don't pay it". While this is a debt that we owe to ourselves it is important to understand that the people that purchase the treasury bills are the ones that we would be affecting. So if we stopped the payments on these loans it would radically affect the holders of this debt this would include our allies such as England, France, Canada, etc. it also includes or trade partners such as Japan, China, and Saudi Arabia. So if they were holding our bonds and we suddenly decided to stop paying interest as promised to the people who bought these debt instruments in good faith and relied upon the US government to make payments in good faith they would have no recourse but to get back at us and all their ways to recoup their losses. This would no doubt include: dumping American dollars, export restrictions, higher oil prices, raising prices on anything to do with the US. Yes so whether we pay interest on our debt, and sell our T-Bills to communists, or we screw everyone over who purchased or T-bills and not pay them the interest they are due there will be serious ramifications. If we do that we will send the price of oil to $500 per barrel to cover their losses and a plastic spatula will cost $50 because of our actions, you and I get to pay for it, , are you going to make your 40 mile one way commute to earn $12.75 an hour before taxes? If gas was $22.50 per gallon? And buy a $2000 microwave to heat up you $175 TV Dinner? So while at first pass it may sound like something we can do the results would be extremely harsh.

Okay so this is been going for 50 years so why is it a problem now, other economists and experts saw the trends and amounts and have screamed the "sky is falling" before and the government hasn't done a thing? Yes people have pointed this out before, but in government it is always easier to go status quo than to make a change. This doesn't mean it's responsible and it doesn't mean it's the best course of action all it meant was that this is the path of least resistance and that I is a politician don't have to take responsibility or accountability for anything which is my prime goal in life. Previous economists who warned of the danger of this much debt were correct and there predictions and totals are valid. In addition there are several other factors outside of our control which I will detail below that will create new challenges for our economy. There are also factors that are fundamentally changing our economy which people who may have said the sky is falling previously didn't have in their argument and unfortunately they can not be avoided.

Our debt payments for 2006 or $550 billion we only paid $400 billion because we borrowed (stole) $150 billion from Social Security. Now with the more people set to retire than ever before for the first time in our country's history we are going to start paying out more in Social Security then we collect. This "little" surplus of $150 billion will be gone, not only will he be gone but were actually going to have to start paying the people who retire. So while we've enjoyed a little surplus while it lasted not only will it quickly now evaporate it will become $150 billion to $500 billion dollars in additional payouts to the first boomers retiring over the next 10 years. This is important because experts put the short full between Social Security and Medicare somewhere between $30 trillion to $120 trillion, from what I've seen on government estimations it's probably double any of these numbers maybe more. More people will be retiring in the next 10 years that have retired in the previous 30 years. Since there is no money in the Social Security's piggyback these funds have to come from you the taxpayer. One thing I can tell you about the government is that they are not hiding money anywhere, they don't have a secret lockbox or a safe deposit box or money in the mattress they don't need any of this because when they need money they just reach into your wallet and take it.

The other shoe that must hit the floor is because of this mass demographic shift of people retiring is that while the number of workers contributing to

Social Security and federal and state taxes will be diminished. Simply put this means less people pay taxes, paying into Social Security, less paying into state taxes, less people contributing to more people retiring. This is a fifth-grade math problem, there is a shortage here the only way the government is going be able to make this difference up is to take more money from the people who are working. That would be you. There is no other place to take money from this should be a concern for all Americans as we head into 2010 and beyond, these are facts not a theory. 50+ million people will begin to retire. So Social Security payment will increase from 7% of the budget to 14% while the workforce reduces by up to 1/3rd. This is another very important factor that we will face that can not be avoided. Less workers, more payees at the same time. There is also no money in "Medicare" ether sometimes this just gets lumped in with Social Security but it is for a different purpose. As we get older we also get more health problems so with this many new retirees the current health care costs which are now rising between 7%-25% could easily double or even more annually. These amounts are not even accounted for. At the same time retirees will also be pulling money which they have saved for retirement out of the stock market, which depending on the market conditions could have a detrimental effect on the economy.

The last point is one about the emerging third world economic might also called 3BC, which stands for 3 billion consumers. China is already a huge trade partner with whom we have a massive trade imbalance, we import for more than we export to China. Analysts say China's economy is growing at almost 18% all the major corporations want to be there and get a piece of this pie. There is little growth in America for mature chain stores. Why have a Home Depot or Target on every street corner to only gain a modicum of growth. When you can be in every town in China as it emerges, wide open unlimited potential. It makes sense and Wall Street loves a good story, you cannot compare the 300 million Americans versus the combined populations of China, Pakistan, India, etc so of course the corporations are courting new fields to plow. Wall St loves growth. This will give these emerging countries 10 times the American buying power in due time over the next 10 to 15 years, investments there will make our treasury notes pale in comparison, would you rather make 2% or 18% on your money. The United States has never had competition as the number one GDP player on the world stage, not only will there be competition we will be in eclipsed tenfold it's just a matter of time. They also will be buying more and more oil and raw materials driving the price up as their economies grow. China already buys half of the steel and concrete made worldwide for their booming construction industry.

Oil purchases for the entire world have been "pegged" to the US dollar which has upheld its value because of the demand for the dollar in order to purchase the life blood of oil one must deal in US dollars. Because of the hostilities with the Muslim culture many OPEC nations are leaning towards a basket of securities instead of the US dollar from which to price oil. As these nations unpeg from the dollar, or the price of petroleum is no longer priced in US dollars the US dollar will fall in value. Kuwait has already unpegged their currency from the dollar and as more countries follow suit the dollar will continue to decrease in buying power throughout the world. The sheer volume of oil purchases alone account for a high percentage of the dollars valuation amongst world currencies if it is no longer the de facto standard to purchase oil it will lose much of its value in the world markets, which will translate to inflation or devaluation either way prices of goods will rise. We have enjoyed stability and less devaluation of our currency because of oil purchases over the last 50 years in US dollars. As an investor would you rather purchase a treasury bond backed by the full faith and credit of the United States government which is in hock up to its eyeballs or a financial instrument backed by oil? This will have a severe impact on our economy.

Consumers have increased their household mortgage and home financing debt from $4.3 Trillion dollars through refinancing to $7.7 Trillion dollars, while at the same time racking up their credit cards. In 2007 US credit card debt total was almost $1 Trillion dollars, which of course is in addition to your mortgage. So Joe Taxpayer does not have any money, so where this money comes from is going to be a problem.

According to government statistics we have a strong diverse economy, with very little or no inflation. Let's take a deeper look.

Government Math (Imaginary numbers)
A consumer price index (CPI) is a statistical estimate of the level of prices of goods and services bought for consumption purposes by households. The change in the CPI is a measure of inflation, and can be used for indexation (or evaluation) of wages, salaries, pensions, or regulated or contracted prices. The CPI is one of several major price indices, and along with the population census and the National Income and Product Accounts, it is one of the most important products of national statistical offices. This number is even further off from reality than GDP.
Tooth Fairy, Easter Bunny and Government Statistics

More Government math, talk about imaginary numbers........

My variation on a theme from the age old Mark Twain quote. Every administration wants to portray low inflation and job growth and GDP growth. The only problem is that these numbers have been adjusted so much they do not reflect reality any longer if they ever did. They measure something but not anything too relevant. Economy is Healthy! Everything is fine. We are told there is very little to no inflation. And that now Wal-Mart accounts for almost 70% of the "basket of goods" for CPI, so if Wal-Mart raises their prices 10% do we now have 7% inflation? Gas and food are not part of the CPI. But real estate is part of GDP. ...Hmmm.... these numbers have been massaged and manipulated until they have lost their meaning.

Gas was $1.46 when Bush got in office it is now $3.25 (and I am being kind) is that not a 50% increase, health care average increase is 15% per year, are your real estate taxes going down? Is Sales tax going down? The minimum wage remained at $5 and we are told that bad things will happen if we raise it. Which is partly true but right now it is just an artificial basement representative of nothing.

So my observation here is that according to government statistics everything is fine. But if I look at John and Jane Middle-America, the median income is $50,000. The median US housing price is $240,000 (up 35% over 7-8 yrs) BUT the median housing price in the top 50 Metro cities where you need to live in order to earn the median income is over $550,000. This represents almost 60% of BOTH incomes before car payments and food, utilities, Ins, Visa, Mastercard, etc, assuming some one gave them the 20% down payment. And I am assuming they both make the median income. Over 50%

earn less and far less. The upper parts of this curve are not "normal people", and I am trying to look at the true majority. Not the CEO for Exxon and a Beverly Hills plastic surgeon and without the uber-rich being blended in.

In contrast to the 1950s and the one breadwinner model working for corporate America, the annual pay was $10,000, but the average home cost was $25,000. Property taxes were non existent, and a car cost under $3,000. Real wages for the middle part of the Bell curve have not kept up with the price of the real things in the world. Normal (non-luxury) cars approach $40,000 a far contrast from them being a fraction of your yearly earnings, they are now on par with a full years tax free salary. But according to the official government story stagnation does NOT exist.

Now two people working full time have less financial strength, less health benefits, and less retirement benefits and less security than our counterparts 30 years ago. And we now work well past the 9 to 5 world because of cell phones, laptops and email. (2 people) We now work 85+ hours vs. a 40 works week for less buying power. Where has the quality of life improved? For the most part Germans get 6 weeks paid vacation each year, Americans take the least vacation time of any industrialized nation.

Government statistics do not point any of this out and while many published stats are useful, for the vast majority of America they have no bearing on reality. Car companies are introducing 6 year loans, and Mortgage companies 40 year, 50 year , 75 year and soon to come 100 year mortgages (as they have in Japan)

Look at these three relatively simple examples and you will see how much is adjusted out of reality that they do no point out.

Lies, damn lies, statistics, and: Hedonics

The manipulation of economic numbers does not stop with GDP. The bureau also began to adjust prices for quality. This practice became known as hedonics. Hedonics adjusts the prices of goods as a result of the increased pleasure a consumer derives from a product. A few examples will illustrate how removed the index has moved away from reality. Tim LaFleur is a commodity specialist for televisions at the BLS. In December last year he adjusted the price of a 27-inch television set for quality improvements. The 27-inch television set had a retail cost of $329.99. However, he decided the new model, which still sold for $329.99, had a better screen. After putting this improvement through the governments complex hedonic adjustment model he determined the improvement in the picture was worth at least $135! Taking in this improvement he adjusted the price of the TV by $135, concluding that the price of the TV had actually fallen by 29%! The price reflected in the CPI was not the actual retail store cost of $329.99, but $194.99. The only problem for we consumers is that if we went to Best Buy or Circuit City to buy that TV, we would still pay $329.99. But in the imaginary basket of goods it is $194.99.

Another example of hedonics at work is the way the BLS treats rising automobile prices. Mr. Reese, a specialist for autos, took a 2005 model car, which went from $17,890 in 2004 to $18,490 in 2005. After adjusting for quality items and making antilock disc brakes standard, the bureau adjusted the actual $600 price increase down by $225. The problem for us consumers is that the price of the car in dealer showrooms was still $18,490.

My personal favorite: Grandma's dresser. If you ever had to help your Grandma or an Aunt or relative move some of their furniture the first thing you would notice is that it was heavy, I mean really heavy the furniture from that era was solid. Furniture made anywhere from around the time of the turn of the century even through the 1940's and 1950's. The second thing you would notice is the craftsmanship, professional carpenters handmade every piece, the drawers all slide well, dovetails sit, backs, bottoms, drawers all thick and wear very well. You might also notice that the furniture is made out of furniture wood, mahogany, oak, cedar, pine, and thick heavy crafted furniture grade wood real wood. Its 50 years old and it still works well. This dresser might have cost Grandma $20 which is $300 in today's worthless dollars. But in the government imaginary basket of goods they put in the $99 dresser 67% less than in the time of your Grandma.

The only difference is that we are measuring something in name only. The piece of shit you get from Target or Ikea and bring home in a flat box is made out of oriented pressboard sheathing, predominately cardboard, sawdust and wax, not mahogany, cedar, or oak, not even plywood. The back is a press on piece of cardboard. The surfaces are a very thin laminate not real wood, certainly not furniture grade drawer fronts like Grandmas dresser. Lastly instead of a professional carpenter skillfully assembling it a buffoon who knows less than nothing about furniture making puts it together for free. This actually takes work, salary, healthcare, and pension away from the skilled labor force. You must also note that you will not hand this dresser down to your kids you will be lucky if you get two years usage before the expert craftsmanship falls apart or if you move it and it still actually works. If you are the government we are talking about an identical substitute for Grandmas dresser for all the rest of us there is reality.

Another often cited example is the refrigerator. "In fact, many consumer goods are much cheaper than they were in the 1970s. A look at 1971 Sears catalog offers a glimpse of some plummeting prices. In 1971, a basic Sears refrigerator cost $399. Adjusted for inflation, that would be about $2,000 in 2005 dollars, or nearly 10 times the $297 price of a basic fridge in today's Sears catalog. Put another way, a fridge costs more than two week's work for an average earner in 1971, but less than two day's labor today." But the $399 refrigerator from 1971 was assembled in Ohio by a factory full of highly skilled American Appliance makers, who earned each $42,000 (1971 equivalent) per year, they had medical benefits and benefits for there families, they had a pension and retirement plan, they had paid vacations they took pride in everything they made. Today's refrigerator is assembled by slaves in Malaysia or China who have never seen a refrigerator and it is shipped here in cargo containers, the workers in Malaysia are not skilled appliance making people. The 1971 refrigerator was considered top on the line; by comparison today's $297 model is an inferior good the "low end model" built especially to push the consumer to a better model every appliance chain and manufacturer uses this strategy, the entire purpose of the $297 model is to push you into the $500 or $600 version or more. The 1971 $399 Refrigerator had a lifetime warranty with in home repair included, in 2005 you can purchase at additional cost a warranty for the refrigerator, and you will be lucky to get 12 months from the manufacturer and another 60 months on an additional warranty much less a lifetime warranty. In 1971 if you did have a problem with the refrigerator you would call the local Sears store and someone would handle your issue personally, today if you have a problem with this appliance you call an 800 number, which rings in another country, where nobody knows who you are or how to help you, or wants to, they may even direct you to another 800 number which rings in a different country. So while we are trying to compare "the same thing" in the refrigerator from 1971 to 2005 at the same time we are not comparing the same thing, you can clearly see that $399 in 1971 dollars does not equal $2000 dollars in 2005 as claimed.

Seasonal adjustments are nothing more than "intervention." They are designed to remove or scale down volatility or price spikes. The only problem is that price spikes never show up in the CPI. Only price drops get recorded. Price spikes are statistically smoothed away so they never show up. Sharp spikes in oil, gasoline, heating oil, or food get statistically adjusted. This keeps the CPI low.

50 Million Americans do not have health care, is this not an indication of a problem? American consumer debt continues to soar. The age for retirement for me has been raised 3 times since I first started working. They post numbers for new job creation, but they fail to point out that

they are for jobs where you could not afford to live from the earnings. There is a huge difference between IBM opening a new office in a town with 500 openings, and Target, Wal-Mart or Starbucks having 500 new positions. The signs are all there but no one in the Government is reading them they are too busy putting out the press release:

"Everything is fine", CPI with a dose of reality

Here are the CPI index numbers adjusted by a real economist to reflect reality.

Isn't it interesting that falling gas prices can push CPI down but the price of gas is not counted in the actual index. (ah, government math) CPI with just hint of reality added does not look 1/100th as rosy as the numbers the government posts every month. Let's take a look at the real numbers for CPI. Remember CPI is the cost of an imaginary basket of services and chances are you will not be able to buy any of the imaginary items in the imaginary basket at a store near you.

Great CPI and Wage information using real numbers:

36 Years of Real US Economic Growth	
Official CPI Rate	Freebuck.com Rate (Reality)
Real Economic Growth (GDP)	
139%	54%
Per Capita Real Economic Growth (GDP)	
62%	3%
Per Worker Real Economic Growth (GDP)	
25%	-19%
Real Wages and Salaries Growth	
108%	34%
Per Capita Real Wage Growth	
40%	-9%
Per Worker Real Wage Growth	
9%	-30%

The chart above is a big reason why the government would try to obscure the true dimensions of the inflation problem. Any widespread belief that inflation and economic growth are improperly reported would have dire consequences on the financial markets and the political environment. I believe that understating the inflation rate is a politically motivated policy that is in place to enable the government to continue to undermine the currency while buying votes through false economics.

"The results shown here about inflation beg the question "Are other government economic statistics also faulty?" In an excellent report by Gillespie Research, Walter J. Williams writes: "As a result of the systemic manipulations, if the GDP methodology of 1980 were applied to today's data, the second quarter's annualized inflation-adjusted GDP growth of 3.0% would be roughly three percent lower (effectively netting to zero percent or below). In like manner, current annual CPI inflation is understated by about 2.7% against the pre-Clinton CPI methodology (would be about 5.7%), and the unemployment rate is understated by about seven percent against its original design and what many people would consider to be actual unemployment (would be about 12.5%). "Williams shows in his report how important economic statistics have been periodically restructured to meet the political needs of those in power. These revisions always make the numbers look more optimistic than reality. The tragedy is that politicians come and go but corrupted statistical methods remain in place long into the future. The net effect of these statistical manipulations is to gradually weaken the quality of reported statistics over time."

Shocking as this maybe the author is really quite conservative and the results he gets are very different and paint a much darker picture than the official Government numbers. His math is reality. The true numbers of real wages, and stagflation are astounding. But show me the $17,000 car and the $260,000 house that he uses in his numbers, even his estimates are too slanted towards conservative.

Milton Friedman one of the greatest Economic minds of the 20th century died at 94
Friedman favored a policy of steady, moderate growth in the money supply, opposed wage and price controls and criticized the Federal Reserve when it tried to fine-tune the economy. A believer in the principles of 18th century economist Adam Smith, he consistently argued that individual freedom should rule economic policy.

In an essay titled "Is Capitalism Humane?" he said that "a set of social institutions that stresses individual responsibility, that treats the individual ... as responsible for and to himself, will lead to a higher and more desirable moral climate."

CPI: The operation was a success but the patient is dead. A tell tale sign that the economy is not a strong as the government portrays. Every Presidential administration tries to put there own special spin on how great the economy is, here is a little tidbit I found (Sept 29 US Census Report) "Americans' savings rate came in at a minus 0.5 percent, compared to a minus 0.7 percent in July. That marked the 17th consecutive month that the savings rate has been in negative territory. That means that Americans are spending all of their after-tax incomes and dipping into savings or borrowing to finance their purchases." The fact that American savings accounts have decreased for 17 consecutive months, does that show anything? Does anyone see economic health in this statistic?
Personal Savings Drop to a 73 year low. People are saving at the lowest level since the Great Depression, and that could be a problem for the millions of baby boomers getting ready to retire. In fact, the Commerce Department reported Thursday that the nation's personal savings rate for all of 2006 was a negative 1 percent, the worst showing in 73 years. I guess this is not an indicator of a weak economy or stagflation. "Everything is Fine."

"I believe that banking institutions are more dangerous to our liberties than standing armies." **Thomas Jefferson**

"Permit me to issue and control the money of a nation, and I care not who makes its laws."
Mayer Amschel Rothschild

The above quote is from the very Wealthy Rothschild Family who is said to have controlled a majority of Europe because of the banking systems that are in place.

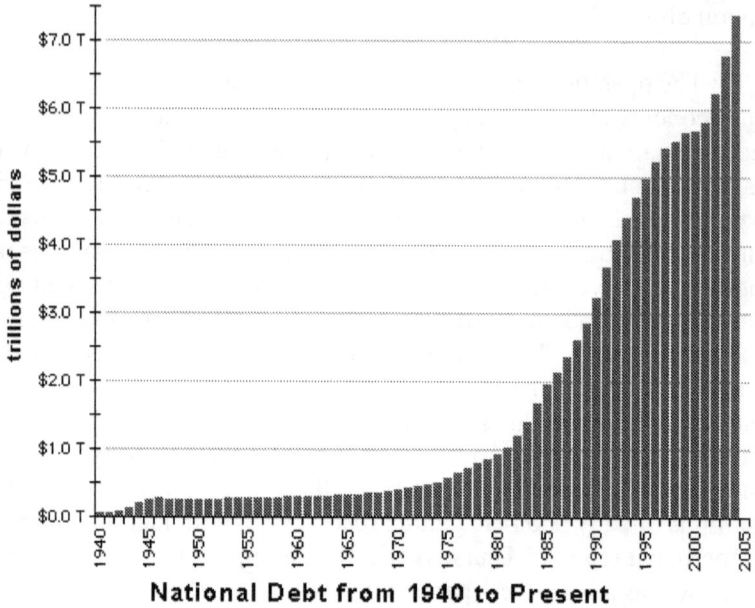

National Debt from 1940 to Present

Source: U.S. National Debt Clock
http://www.brillig.com/debt_clock/

The National Debt $40,000 per every man woman and child in America +
(Iraq costs)

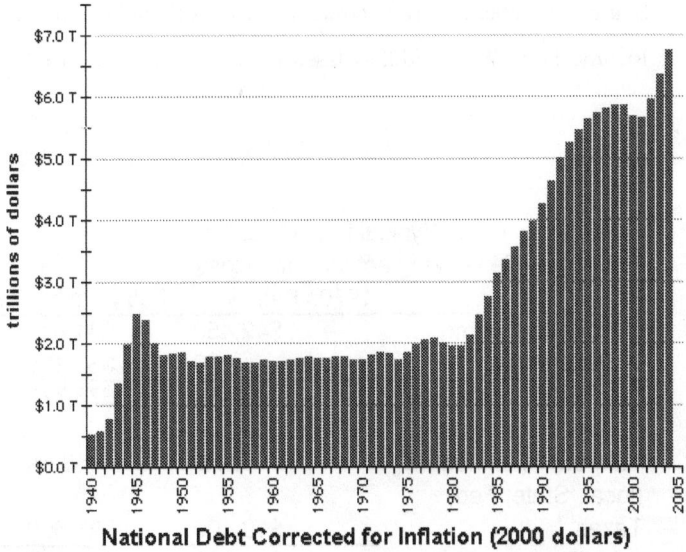

National Debt Corrected for Inflation (2000 dollars)

Source: U.S. National Debt Clock
http://www.brillig.com/debt_clock/

Notice a trend?

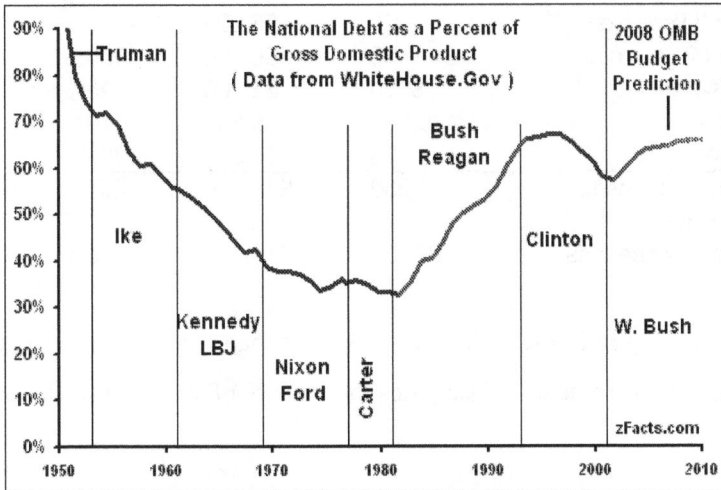

The National Debt as a Percent of Gross Domestic Product (Data from WhiteHouse.Gov)

It is "way more cooler" as a percentage of GDP but does not reflect interest payments nor what would happen if you doubled or tripled interest rates.

Also remember part of GDP is the governments MasterCard.

http://zfacts.com/p/318.html

Source: Elizabeth Warren, co-author with Amelia Warren Tyagi of "The Two-Income Trap: Why Middle-Class Mothers and Fathers Are Going Broke"

Comparing 1970s "typical family" vs. 2005
How 2 people working actually have less

	1970s Family	2005 Family	% Change
Husbands Income	$42,450	$41,670	-2%
Wifes Income	$0	$32,100	1000%
Total Family Income	$43,450	$73,770	74%
Tax rate % of income (local, State, Fed)	24%	32%	33%
Taxes	$10,400	$23,600	127%
After Tax Income	$32,050	$50,170	56%
Major Fixed Expenses			
Home Mortgage	$5,820	$10,250	76%
Day Care 8 year old	$0	$6,000	1000%
PreSchool 2 year old	$0	$6,960	1000%
Health Insurance	$900	$2,200	145%
Automobile 1	$5,000	$5,500	10%
Automobile 2	$0	$5,000	1000%
Total Fixed Expenses	$11,950	$35,910	200%
Total Income after tax and Expenses	$20,400	$14,260	**-30%**

2 people working full time in 2005 to make less than 1 person in 1970 but according to Government CPI statistics there is no inflation or stagflation.

DESTROYING AMERICA

Chapter 3   The War Machine or "This is Sparta!"

The next American addiction: guns. In 2006 United States spent $522 billion on defense over 20% of our annual budget, please note this does not include the $900 billion set aside for the conflict in Iraq and Afghanistan. If one were to look objectively at the United States as an outside observer a person might think that the United States was preparing for war like ancient Rome, on a daily basis, and to be at war with the entire world. The United States spends more on the Department of Defense than all of the next 18 US state departments combined, including the Department of the Interior, Department of Education, Department of Health and Human Services and the next 15 other governmental departments, combined. While having a strong military is important we do have to ask ourselves why is that department need more money than every other department in the government added together and if so why?

To put this in proper perspective if we assume that we could be in some sort of upcoming conflict with China or Russia we spent 7 to 10 times more than both of these countries on weapons, China spent $63 billion in 2006 in the United States was at $522 billion. There could be somewhat of a knee-jerk reaction because of 9/11 but that is not the total cause, there has not been a time since 1990 when the defense budget has dipped below $350 billion per year, this is Sparta! We have been preparing for war without having a rival. We spent more on Defense than the next 15 countries highest defense budgets combined.

And here's where it gets kind of strange in 2006 there was about $1 trillion spent worldwide on defense but the United States accounted for half of all military spending in the entire world, why are we spending 50% of all the money for weapons expenditures when we have 6% of the population. This is why to an outside observer one might make the case that we're nuts this really is Sparta were bringing back the Roman Republic and the Coliseum will reopen on Friday nights maybe with a pay-per-view event. One may ask why would a sane; peace loving country spends 50% of all the money spent in the entire world on weapons for 6% (300 Million citizens out of 6 Billion people worldwide) of the population? While part of this is because of the Iraq conflict, Al Qaeda and the "War on Terror" one cannot solely lay the blame on these issues since the spending goes way, way back to before 9/11. In many ways it seems that the Cold War with Communist Russia never ended for the United States.

Now if another nation was doing this we would be gravely concerned about what they're doing and why they're spending this kind of money on weapons, we would be the first to ask on the floor of the UN: Hey, you only have 300 million people why are you spending half a $1 trillion dollars on bombs, but if it is us doing it then it's okay. We would call that country with 6% of the population and spending 50% of the world totals for arms a hostile, war-mongering nation, they might even get added to the Axis of Evil. We would launch a satellite into orbit immediately to watch their ass 24x7. We can no longer spend money as if we were fighting World War III and WW4 and WW5 at the same time. And unlike some other government spending which may be marginal or partially unneeded like a road, or a bridge or a building obviously a bomb or missile have but one purpose and are never going to be used unless they're needed and if they're needed it's probably not for a good thing.

To put this into proper perspective even during or at the end of the Cold War we were spending around $300 Billion dollars (in 1990 dollars) to safe guard our country against Communist Russia. So over the years the Department of Defenses budget was largely based on the classic Cold War threat of a global superpower with full nuclear capabilities, protecting us from a nation of 200+ million Russians, 6,000 to possibly as many as 40,000 nuclear weapons, a huge standing army, first strike submarines, satellites, long range bombers and Intercontinental Ballistic Missiles (ICBMs). In addition we had a deployment for NATO. Compare this with today a few hundred thousand committed terrorists who used a 747 as a poor mans missile. Why do we need 2 and 3 times the money to be safe from a group of people that have no military capabilities? No missiles, no tanks, no fighter planes. Hating us is one thing, hating us and having an aircraft carrier is quite another, and they do not have one.

The US military budget was 29 times as large as the combined spending of the six rogue states Cuba, Iran, Libya, North Korea, Sudan and Syria along with the axis of evil. Six potential enemies including Russia and China totaled to 30% of the US military budget. Many people will talk about the latest bogeyman and tell you that you have to have a strong defense and while that is true having a strong defense and spending half a $1 trillion are two different things we are not fighting World War III. We can no longer afford defense spending as if we were in an arms race with Cold War Russia the only people that benefit here are defense contractors but if you say that you are un-American and you are not a patriot. You can call names if you like but the answer is that we need less $2 million missiles, less $400 hammers, and less $300 toilet seats and not whether we can spend $522 billion but why are we spending anywhere near $522 billion?

In addition we are the world's largest arms dealer and if what is past is prologue we have seen our allies turn on us and used our own equipment against us, Saddam Hussein's antipersonnel mines were American, Iran fought Iraq with American weapons, and Oliver North was embroiled in Iran-Contra arms for drugs scandal, these are certainly things we don't wish to foster and continue. And please note this does not bring into account any black bag projects and off budget items such as Area 51 which does not exist. The Department of Defense budget is slated for $627 Trillion dollars in 2007, and another $625 Billion in 2008 not including the Iraq-Afghanistan conflict currently weighing in at and additional $900+ Billion dollars. (Or CBO estimate of $2.4 Trillion dollars through 2017,with no end in sight)

Moreover there is no correlation to the amount of dollars spent and the safety or security of the United States, this has been and continues to be a fallacy. In 1990 after the Cold War ended, and during the time when Clinton was President an average of $350 billion was spent every year, year after year on defense, add to that the budgets for the FBI, CIA, NSA and various other alphabet soup divisions of the government and you will see that by the time September 2001 rolled around we had spent between $5 and $7 trillion dollars in the name of security. But none of this prevented 9/11 from happening. We have been in Iraq for 5 years and as of the time of writing this no one knows why. No one knows if there is any positive benefit and only time will tell as of right now it just looks like Vietnam but a lot worse. We have created a weakened nation engaged in a civil war in the middle of the most hostile, volatile region in the world. Its not about quantity its about quality Al Qaeda and the Taliban both got part of this funding too, so more is not better.

As a matter of fact let us take a look at one of our allies Saudi Arabia. We have been allies with the Saudis since World War 2 and since they make so much money from the oil trade it seems the US capitalist thing to do is to sell them something and get some of that money back. So selling them weapons to help keep them safe seems the very American thing to do. They are buying an average of $15 billion dollars total of arms per year from multiple countries. The Saudis are considered such a close ally that there have been probes and investigation by the US, Britain, France and other countries into both unauthorized purchases and non-market items. A non-market item are weapons which we do not export or sell to anyone but somehow the Saudis were able to buy them. This means the Saudis have a lot of really great US military weapons in their arsenal. The Saudis also bought some really great weaponry from other countries as well, so they have amassed a great arsenal. But what do we know about these people? As far as I can tell you there is no voting, womens rights are non-existent, and there is no freedom of religion, they hold beheadings in their town square. The government is little more than a dictatorship but a very wealthy one. What would prevent a coup by a faction within their country from seizing power? And taking control of the military? Or a group within the military starting a revolution? Because it has not happened, does not mean it will not happen. If you thought Osama Bin Laden did some damage with commercial airliners imagine when he gets a hold of all this gear, F-16s, tomahawks, cruise missiles, Abrams tanks. For those that say it will not happen we backed the Shah of Iran for 25 years and he loved American weapons too.

President Eisenhower, in his final address to the nation before leaving office in 1961, issues a rather extraordinary warning to the American people that the country "must guard against unwarranted influence, whether sought or unsought, by the military-industrial complex. The potential for the disastrous rise of misplaced power exists and will persist." Remember Eisenhower was a decorated General in World War 2 (WW2) and he is telling us about the dangerous of the military-industrial-complex maybe we should have listened to him. Isn't this the strangest source for this advice?

So what would the crafters of the Constitution our forefathers think about this? Well right in the Declaration of Independence they warn about the danger of standing armies so a big military is not high on the list of recommendations. Part of the right to bear arms comes from their mistrust of government. And the forefathers never envisioned a time where troops could board a plane and be anywhere in 24 hours, nor that one man could push a button and blow up an entire country thousands of miles away, let alone they believed that a standing army was not a good thing. So the US spending more on Defense than the rest of the entire budget combined would not be a positive thing to our forefathers. Many people will think well these government contracts create jobs but overpaying for things that you do not need will never be a lasting condition. We need more people working on a cure for cancer and less people making bombs and aircraft carriers. The government could reallocate those funds back to the private sector through initiatives, tax breaks, incentives, etc. Part of the money should go to renewable energy but by and large if we cut the defense budget in half, then cut your taxes by whatever amount correlates to the reduction. This could easily be 10% of your taxes.

What we currently have is a situation that will qualify for a replacement scenario for the Cold War, we are "War with Terror" and with radical Islamic terrorists. This fulfills all the criteria and will obviously take a lot of time, will have no tangible results, and will have no measurable progress, but the best part is it will cost trillions of dollars as the "radical Muslims" (Islamo-fascists) replace the "bad Russians" in the spy books. This current bogeyman is set to justify any means necessary in spending to fight a new form of the Crusades, the only thing they need is your fear. They need to make and keep you afraid of the latest bogeyman or they will have no reason to spend $522 Billion dollars (and $625 Billion more in 2007) so keep watching CNN and be scared, while the rest of the world watches us and tries to figure out why we are spending half a trillion dollars on weapons for 6% of the worlds population and if they are our next target for exporting Democracy.

The defense spending is the largest budget item next to the interest payments on the national debt, the more this amount can be reduced the more the reduction on the total federal budget can be reduced, there is no reason the Department of Defense budget could not be pushed back to 1990s levels of spending, $350 Billion dollars, it has had enough of "seasonal lift" and needs to be reduced. Reducing the largest item on the budget will have the most fiscal impact. Getting the Department of Defense in line with reducing the overall size of government is a much needed step because of how much they account for in the budget, the boom years are over.

Naturally the common people don't want war: Neither in Russia, nor in England, nor for that matter in Germany. That is understood. But, after all, it is the leaders of the country who determine the policy and it is always a simple matter to drag the people along, whether it is a democracy, or a fascist dictatorship, or a parliament, or a communist dictatorship. ... Voice or no voice, the people can always be brought to the bidding of the leaders. That is easy. All you have to do is tell them they are being attacked, and denounce the peacemakers for lack of patriotism and exposing the country to danger. It works the same in any country.   (Sounds like this could have been said last week.)

— General Herman Goering, President of German Reichstag and Nazi Party, Commander of Luftwaffe during World War II, April 18, 1946. (This quote is said to have been made during the Nuremburg Trials, but in fact, while during the time of the trials, was made in private to an Allied intelligence officer, later published in the book, Nuremburg Diary.)

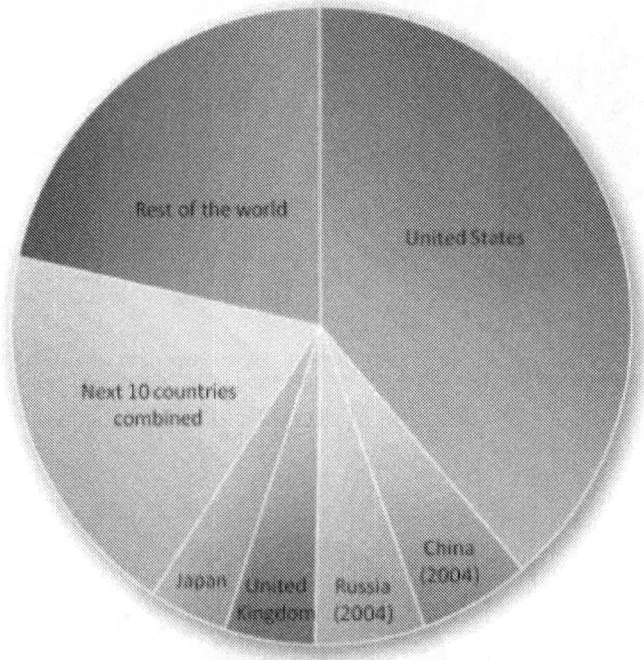

Global Distribution of Military Expenditure in 2005

Rest of the world

United States

Next 10 countries combined

Japan

United Kingdom

Russia (2004)

China (2004)

Source: Center for Arms Control and Non-Proliferation, 2007

Military Expenditures by Country 2005

Allocation of US 2006 Taxes

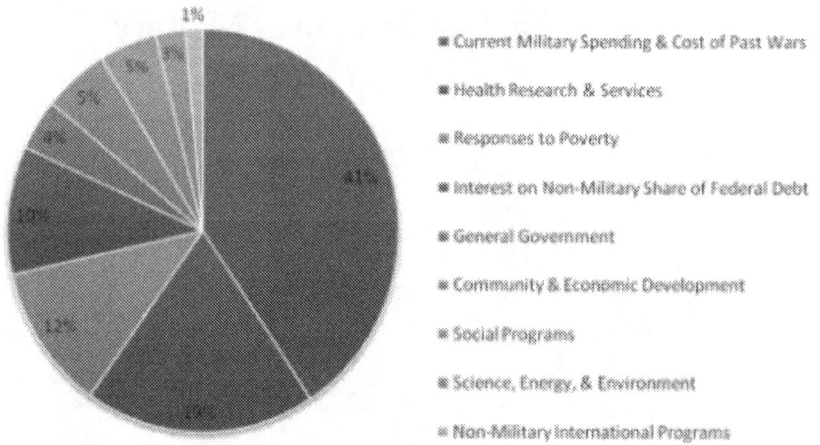

- Current Military Spending & Cost of Past Wars
- Health Research & Services
- Responses to Poverty
- Interest on Non-Military Share of Federal Debt
- General Government
- Community & Economic Development
- Social Programs
- Science, Energy, & Environment
- Non-Military International Programs

Source: Friends Committee on National Legislation, February 2007

Allocation of every Tax Dollar collected

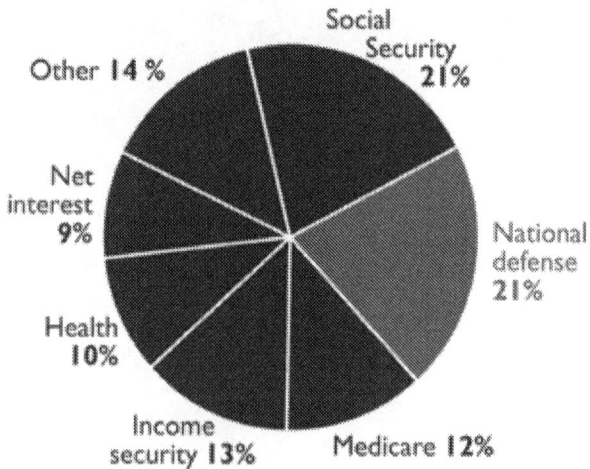

Source: *Washington Post* , Feb.   Military Spending as a percentage of all Government spending.

	2006 (in billions of dollars)	2006 percent of federal funds budget
Current Military Spending	571.6	28%
Cost of Past Wars	263.5	13%
Total military percent		41%
Health Research & Services	393.5	19%
Responses to Poverty	241.0	12%
Interest on Non-Military Share of Federal Debt	211.5	10%
General Government	84.6	4%
Community & Economic Development	112.1	5%
Social Programs	97.7	5%
Science, Energy, & Environment	50.8	2%
Non-Military International Programs	29.8	1%

Percent dollars spent as percentage of the entire US Budget

Military spending in 2005   ($ Billions, and percent of total)

Military spending in 2005 ($ Billions, and percent of total)

Country	Dollars (billions)	% of total	Rank
United States	420.7	43%	1
China *	62.5	6%	2
Russia *	61.9	6%	3
United Kingdom	51.1	5%	4
Japan	44.7	4%	5
France	41.6	4%	6
Germany	30.2	3%	7
India	22	2%	8
Saudi Arabia	21.3	2%	9
South Korea	20.7	2%	10
Italy	17.2	2%	11
Australia	13.2	1%	12

"I know war as few other men now living know it, and nothing to me is more revolting. I have long advocated its complete abolishment, as its very destructiveness on both friend and foe has rendered it useless as a method of settling international disputes."
Douglas MacArthur

"For 45 years of the Cold War we were in an arms race with the Soviet Union. Now it appears we're in an arms race with ourselves."
Admiral Eugene Carroll, Jr., U.S. Navy,
Vice President Emeritus
Center for Defense Information

World Military Expenditure

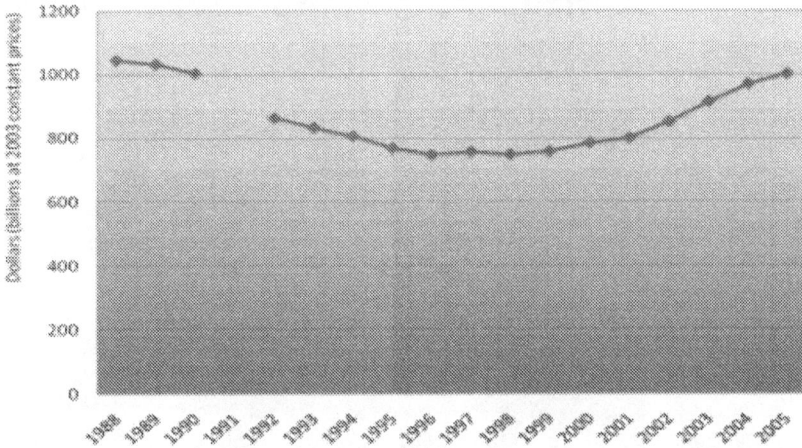

Source: Stockholm International Peace Research Institute Yearbook 2006

World Military Spending, 2004

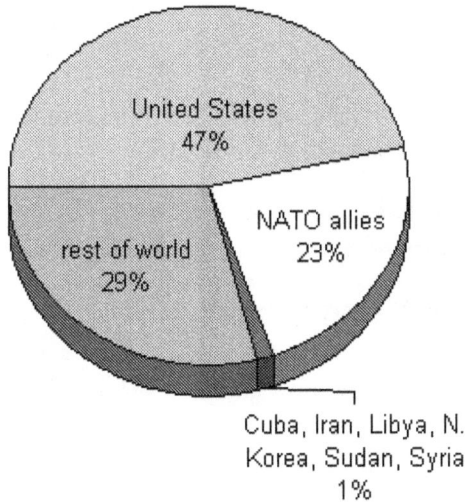

United States
47%

NATO allies
23%

rest of world
29%

Cuba, Iran, Libya, N.
Korea, Sudan, Syria
1%

© 2005 National Priorities Project, Inc.

//borgenproject.org/Defense_Spending.html

US Military Expenditure since 1998

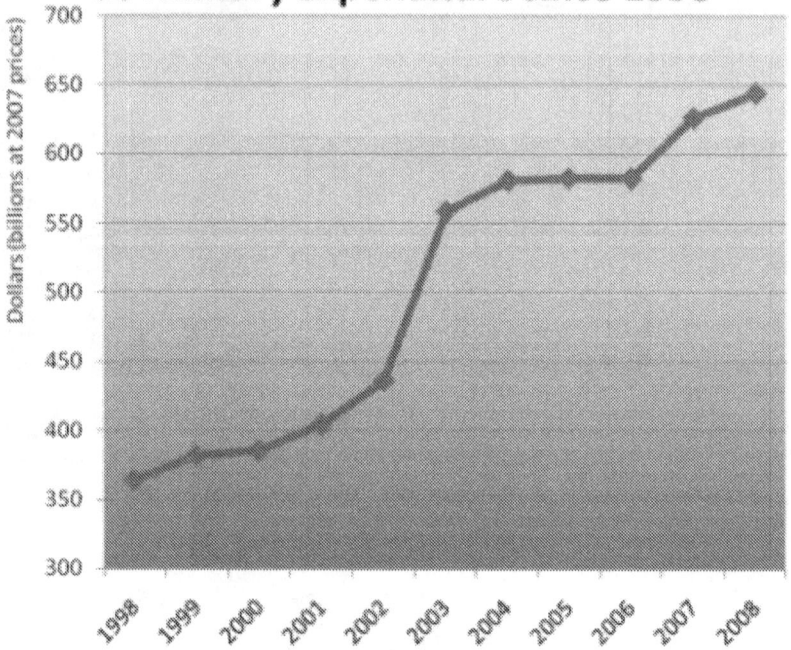

Dollars (billions at 2007 prices)

700
650
600
550
500
450
400
350
300

1998 1999 2000 2001 2002 2003 2004 2005 2006 2007 2008

Sources: Friends Committee on National Legislation, Center for Arms Control and Non-Proliferation, 2006, 2007.

See important notes about data in accompanying table

Annual Military Expenditures US

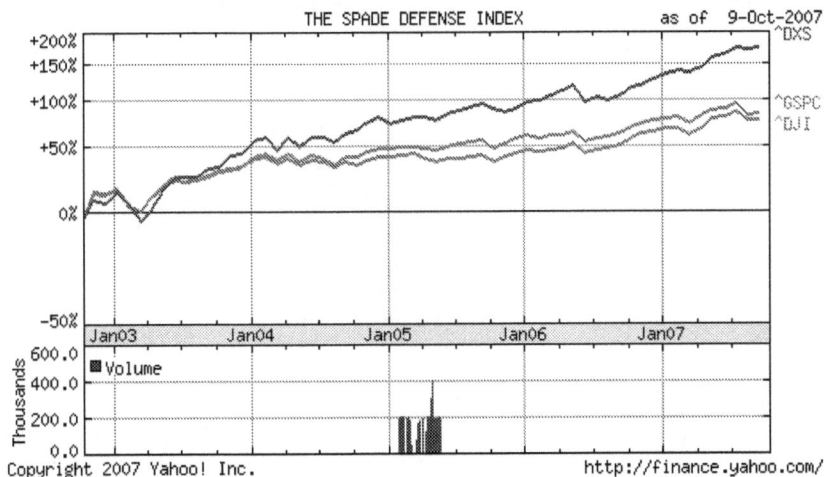

THE SPADE DEFENSE INDEX   as of   9-Oct-2007

Copyright 2007 Yahoo! Inc.   http://finance.yahoo.com/

How DEFENSE INDUSTRY Stocks fared vs. the Market in general

http://www.spadeindex.com/components.html

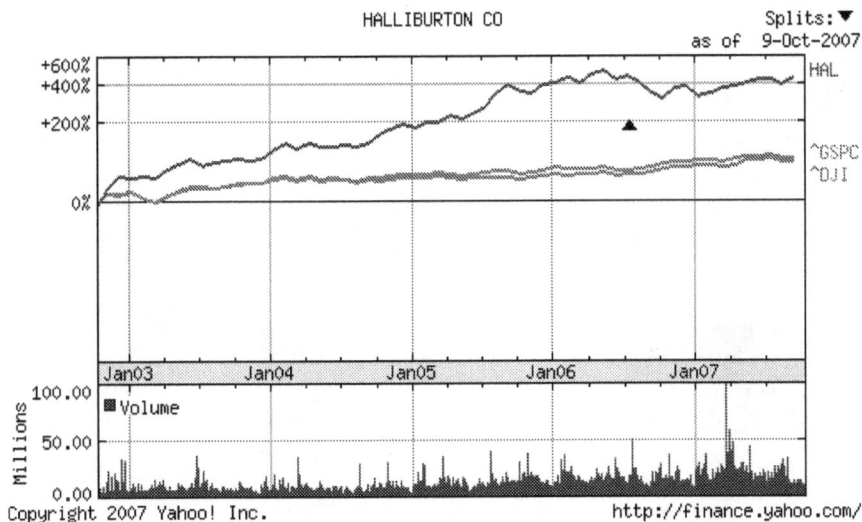

HALLIBURTON CO   Splits:▼
as of   9-Oct-2007

Copyright 2007 Yahoo! Inc.   http://finance.yahoo.com/

DESTROYING AMERICA

Chapter 4   The Size of Government

Since every employee working for the government adds to the overall burden or total overhead of government, the more we do to control the number of government employees the more we do to minimize the cost of government. Moreover a liberal or conservative economist will tell you that productivity, and total return from a government building or employee will never equal the output or return from its counterpart in the private sector, (and may actually be a negative number) but they both draw from the same talent and resource pool. A park never makes money, nor a library, or prison etc

Are you on the payroll?

'Least government is best' - Thomas Jefferson

The systems of Socialism and Communism are partly defined by the fact that the country is by and large run by and controlled by the government and in those models a vast majority of the population in fact work for the government. So the government exerts a very large amount of control on the populace. Even mentioning the words Communism or Socialism (especially in the McCarthy Era) was enough to cause people distress, the US is a free country run by the people. But the more I researched how many people work for the government the more I found until hitting a paradox. I have come across some troubling employment data. My rhetorical question is: at what percentage do you qualify for a majority? 5%, 10%, 20%, 30%? And if so Where does "Capitalism" stop? And Socialism? Or Corporatism? Begin?

In researching how the national debt got to be what it is, the answer was easy: government spending. So then I was looking for a reason why government spending is spiraling out of control, and hey I found it. It's because of government. The reason is government, government and even more government, with extra government on the side. More government programs, more government projects, more government buildings, more government pensions, more government spending and this does not even include the "peace" in Iraq. Oh yes and more helpful government employees, federal, state, local, county, you can never have enough government employees. And WE pay for every single one, twice. There is also the job security benefit which no one in the private sector can claim.

For comparison sake here are the largest employers in the US, Wal-Mart is the largest domestic employer with over 1,200,000 Employees in the US. UPS has 400,000, McDonalds 450,000, Siemens 460,000 (Worldwide) Daimler Chrysler 380,000 (worldwide)
How many government employees do you think there are? Don't look down and cheat,
pick a number first: 1 Million ? 2 million?, 3 million ? 4 million?
5 million......

So how many people work in government? (work = funded by)
2 Million Full Time Federal Employees
2 Million Military (higher right now)
1 Million Postal
13 Million Jobs from Fed contracts, grants, regulatory, conservation (direct

funding and creation of jobs)* many jobs have been eliminated by Clinton only to be recreated in the private sector with a 10-99 for the same position but as an "outside contractor", but the government is writing the check.

Sub Total 18 Million but wait….there are: +

18.5 Million State, Local, City, County, Fire, Police, Port, Corrections, DMV, Teachers, etc, etc

2.3 Million people in prison (guests of the state) we are paying for this

15 Million (missiles, tanks etc these are jobs directly related to fed GDP spend)*

5 Million Above portion of jobs directly related to health care based on the percentage + education

Sub Total 40.8 Million …Lets not forget… +

5 Million Welfare recipients

560,000 Unemployed

Grand Total 64.4 Million "jobs" (people being funded by US Gov)

US Work force was 140 M in 2001, US Census, I am adjusting upwards to 145 Million

44.5% of the people employed in the US work for the government whether they know it or not.

Does 44% represent a majority? Does this resemble capitalism? Laissez-Faire system?

Milton Friedman acknowledged that "pure capitalism" did not exist, but said that nations that cherished freedom must strive to keep the economy as close to the ideal as possible.

He said government should allow the free market to operate to solve inflation and other economic problems. - Milton Friedman Nobel Prize Economics, Chancellor University of Chicago School of Business, Advisor to 3 Presidents. A believer in the principles of 18th century economist Adam Smith, he consistently argued that individual freedom should rule economic policy.

You wonder why there are so many taxes and why they are so high, you do the math here. One person out of two of "us" needs to pay for the both of us and that person is you. Even if you completely disagree with my research and spending allocations so you cut the number in half does that look right to you? 25% of the work force is employed by Big Brother. I actually could not believe the number when I first saw them. Technically my number is conservative 13% of the workforce are employed because of compliance issues alone that's almost 19M people I included only half.

Should we add the 45.4 Million Social Security recipients to the list?, when the boomers retire this number will become almost 70 Million by 2020. I will leave this off for now. But technically they are on the payroll, but not part of the "workforce".

20% of the US GDP is spent by the government, and almost another 13% of GDP is spent on compliance that is where the * notes comes from. The 20% consists of everything from Mars Lander parts, bridges, concrete, sand, tanks, Hubble Telescope, paper clips, ink, staplers, pens, missiles, $400 hammers, $300 toilet seats, computers, satellite parts, etc, your check may not say US Government but the source of the funding is.

These employee numbers do not reflect the current higher employee count for the Military, DoD and contractors due to the Iraqi conflict such that the data would not be skewed. This does NOT include military reservists, disabled, or pensions. K-12 Teachers are included as they work for the school system, TSA, Homeland Security, IRS, BATF, DIA, FBI, CIA, NSA, DEA, customs, INS, Corrections, Border Patrol, Consulate, Embassy, all military branches and Coast Guard, Federal, State, County, Port, City, Local, Municipal, State Universities, Courts, are included.

Almost 40% of "us" have a vested interest in voting for things to make government bigger, expanding programs and higher spending, creating job security and new positions for themselves and perpetuating the status quo of government. And this 40% number will only move in one direction. Now I start to see why nothing gets done and although there are intelligent people in Government the outcome is always the same.

Simplistic, yes. FACTUAL, yes. But it helps make a serious point. 40% of the workforce being overhead is a serious problem, this is a super-majority. This begs the question what would our founding fathers think. The guys who thought debt was the pathway to hell. The guys that believed that that the government should not interfere with trade. People like Ben Franklin, Thomas Malthus and Adam Smith who said the "invisible hand" will guide the market, not the hand of government. The policy of Laissez-Faire, or "hands off" was a guiding principle of our country, seems we took a hard left turn somewhere.

'Least government is best' - Thomas Jefferson

For the Record Mussolini referred to his government model and society as "Corporatism"

I have painted a picture here with very broad strokes so whether this is completely accurate or not it really does not matter as much as the realization that the era where we can have 40% of the workforce working in some capacity for the government is over. All this overhead puts an additional burden on every worker, creates endless procedures, and new heights of administrivia. More employees, more policies, more taxes and more complexity is not the answer and it is not where our future lies. While it may not be politically correct to say this more police, more DMV and more court clerks are not going to solve anything, they will only be an additional slice out of your paycheck. We do not need to be paying for more people whose quality of work can not be measured that can never be fired. There is also an additional overhead on most civil employees because you are paying Social Security for them but most also receive a pension so even when they retire there is a burden on their organization which we still pay for. People that never come off payroll and can never be fired perfect we need more of them. Less employees and less lifetime pensions lowers the burden on all of us.

What is more disturbing than the sheer number of public employees is the growth of government employees vs. the growth of the population of the United States. While the population has grown by about 110% in the last 50 years, public sector employees have grown 470% in the same period. There were 2.3 Local public employees per 100 citizens, we now have 6.4 local public employees per 100 citizens but a fair question would be why? Why in an age of automation, computerization, modernization and tremendous leaps in productivity why would it take 3 times the people to do the same things? For example if you called city hall in 1960 and asked: "how much are my property taxes", they probably could not put you on hold, they would put the phone down, they might have to walk down the hall or downstairs or even into another building, find the right box, look for your property, address, look for the physical folder, write down the information, then walk back and give you your answer this might surely take a few minutes or longer, no fax machines, and if you need a copy they have to mail it. Nowadays this entire query would take 6-10 seconds, that is if you wanted to speak with a human, you would give your name and address and the information would pop up on the screen and they would give you the answer. So the productivity is up by a factor of 100+ (1000??) so why triple the workforce?

The DMV does not need more people it needs simpler processes, all of these organizations have grown by self perpetuation, the more complex the more employees the higher the payroll the bigger the budget the more power they have. Imagine if the 9,000 page US tax code was 1 page, something like this: take amount earned last year and multiply by 10%, pay this amount. More money is lost in the 100,000 employees of the IRS than whatever extra amount is gleaned in their arcane fascist loophole laden hyperbole. Special interests also poke in their ugly head. Gray Davis the former Governor of California spent more money on prisons than he did on education. In California prison guard unions were the number one contributor to the election campaigns of former governor Gray Davis, under whom California's spending on prisons increased by hundreds of millions of dollars per year. They all voted for him, he paid Billions of dollars for shiny new prisons to be built and fully staffed. Davis spent over $5 Billion on prisons in CA during the last 5 years of his term, he spent $600M for one prison alone, and $1.2 Billion dollars to add 9000 beds another year. Bigger budgets more power. All in the guise of being tough on crime.

Now I know we need prisons, but I don't know that we need $12 Billion dollars worth of prisons, maybe it is indicative that something else is not working very well. We have a huge budget to hide our mistakes but none to fix them.

Zero Base Budgeting

So rather than continue a status quo operational model such as taking last years budget and increasing it by 10% from now until the end of time, we should do the opposite take last years budget and reduce it by 10%. But zero base asks an even harder question take a look at every single budget item and ask why do you need it at all? Don't assume you need 10% more or 10% less do you need any? Can we cut this item 70%? In the private sector there are valid reasons for last years budget + X% there are measurable tangible objectives. This is much harder in the public sector with intangible and harder to measure results, harder but not impossible. Growth in the public sector should not be a goal. Moreover this is why wool farmers had subsidies after World War 2 ended, we needed wool for blankets but then it became an entitlement and an entire division of the Department of Agriculture, same with bee keepers and I'm not singling out farmers there a re so many of these programs that need to be eradicated that zero base budgeting is the smartest way to go. Archer Daniels Midland (ADM) is a $40B company that gets some of the same subsidies that a small family farmer would get and I don't think they need the help.

Jefferson wrote ""I place economy among the first and most important of republican virtues, and public debt as the greatest of the dangers to be feared."

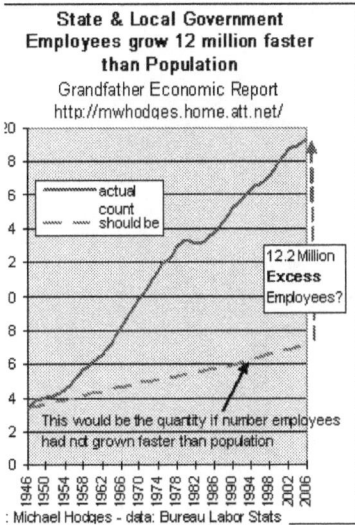

State & Local Government Employees grow 12 million faster than Population
Grandfather Economic Report
http://mwhodges.home.att.net/

actual count
should be

12.2 Million **Excess** Employees?

This would be the quantity if number employees had not grown faster than population

: Michael Hodges - data: Bureau Labor Stats

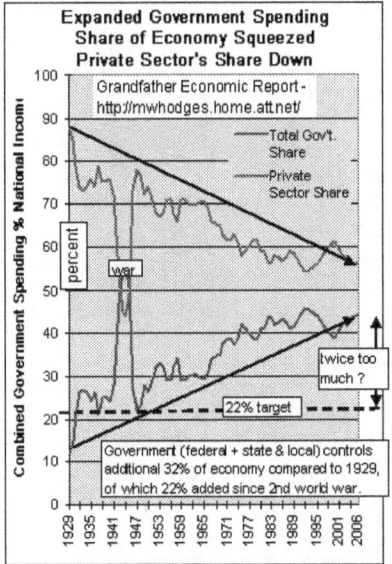

Expanded Government Spending Share of Economy Squeezed Private Sector's Share Down
Grandfather Economic Report - http://mwhodges.home.att.net/

Total Gov't. Share
Private Sector Share

war

twice too much ?

22% target

Government (federal + state & local) controls additional 32% of economy compared to 1929, of which 22% added since 2nd world war.

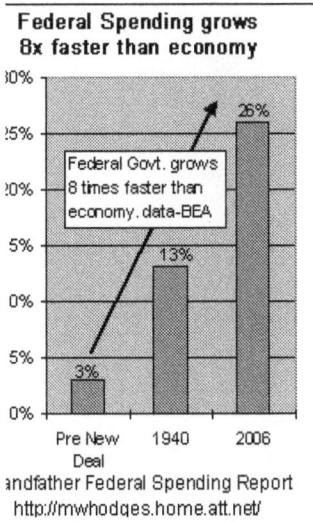

Federal Spending grows 8x faster than economy

Federal Govt. grows 8 times faster than economy. data-BEA

26%

13%

3%

Pre New Deal | 1940 | 2006

andfather Federal Spending Report
http://mwhodges.home.att.net/

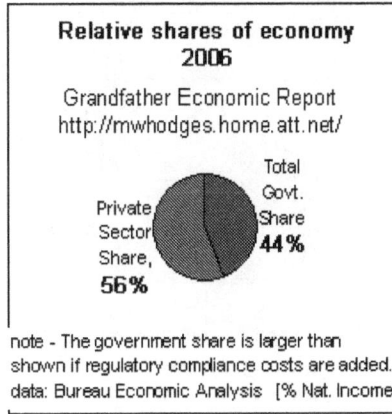

Relative shares of economy 2006

Grandfather Economic Report
http://mwhodges.home.att.net/

Total Govt. Share 44%

Private Sector Share, 56%

note - The government share is larger than shown if regulatory compliance costs are added.
data: Bureau Economic Analysis [% Nat. Income]

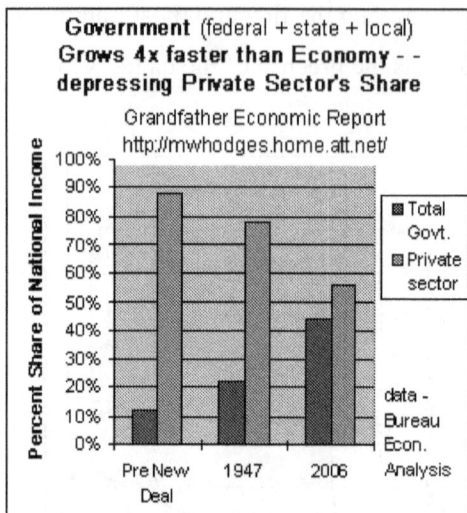

Government (federal + state + local)
Grows 4x faster than Economy - -
depressing Private Sector's Share

Grandfather Economic Report
http://mwhodges.home.att.net/

data - Bureau Econ. Analysis

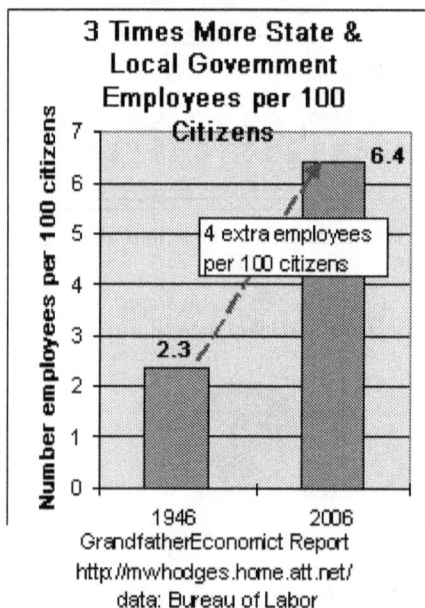

3 Times More State & Local Government Employees per 100 Citizens

6.4

4 extra employees per 100 citizens

2.3

1946   2006

GrandfatherEconomict Report
http://mwhodges.home.att.net/
data: Bureau of Labor

http://www.bls.gov/news.release/empsit.nr0.htm

22.233M of 137.864M is 16%, how many business services and service providing roles should be included, similarly 16% of Health and Education positions are de facto for government workers.

DESTROYING AMERICA

Chapter 5 – Campaign Finance Reform – or
Who Does Your Congressman Work For?

Well even if we control spending, manage the debt and balance the budget we will still fall right back into bad habits because of the method we use to select our politicians. Campaign finance reform is the 3rd leg of the 3 legged stool and if we do not change the way we finance people who run for office we will go right back into debt, and spending and broken budgets because of the process of how we elect our candidates and who controls them. Have you made a $1 million dollar campaign contribution to a candidate? Who do you think has clout with a Congressman or Senator. Have you made a $100,000 dollar contribution to a candidate? $10,000 contribution? How about $1000? What are the chances of the candidate taking your phone call and versus taking the phone call of a $10,000+ contributor?

For a moment lets pretend we were in 6th grade and post a question to try to better understand this existing process, what does a $1 million campaign contribution actually buy someone anyway? You see in the America political system giving the candidate $1 million dollars is considered a bribe and both the giver and the receiver can be given big fines and jailed, however if you make a $1 million dollar contribution to the candidates campaign that is 100% legal. Confused? So you may ask what is the difference between giving the candidate money and giving the candidate a "campaign" contribution, and the answer is that one of those contributions is legal and tax deductable and the other is not and can give you jail time.

Some call this influence, clout, access, some a bribe, or dirty tainted money but what ever you may call it this is a normal part of our existing American political process. Like it or not this is what is going on all the time in Washington, this is a normal part of the day to day environment. If this built-in corrupt process does not make sense to you why would you keep it?

This is the other reason why our political system has gone awry; we have a process in place that makes our elected officials basically prostitutes for lack of a better word. Regardless of party affiliation campaign contributions are the life blood of every candidate this is the currency of Washington and this dirty money comes from special interests, corporations and PAC funds (political action committee funds) Corruption and influence are built right into the system that's why we get such abhorrent results from our elected officials they only spend part of their time pandering to their constituents they spend a majority of their time pandering to big donors because they have to. The big donors are very happy to "donate" but there is always a hidden cost attached. The Corporations love this process they can make $10 million dollars in legal, tax deductable campaign contributions and get loopholes passed that will save them billions of dollars and cost you thousands of dollars more each year. There is no other place around other than a horse racing track where such a small investment can pay off this big. The Corporations are very smart too, they give to both sides so whichever side wins they have access. In essence we have built a machine that even if the politician has the best intentions and wants no part of the "Washington game" he can not escape it, he or she is forced into the dirty donor game if they want to stay in office. Are these the kinds of people we want representing us? Why would we want to continue this dirty, sordid process? Looking at the results of our government one can clearly see that it is a broken corrupt process. This makes for an unrepresentative democracy which is not by the people for the people but only for those with big checkbooks.

So public funding is obviously the answer, and the next question then becomes how much will this cost me? It will cost you much less than what the current shady politics and dirty back door deals cost you. And rather than reinvent the wheel I found some great information at a campaign reform website aptly titled Just six dollars ($6). (just6dollars.org) Candidates chase and court large donors rather than communicate with voters because they have to. Leaders waste precious time and energy catering to lobbyists, special interests, corporate sponsors and large donors, continuously raising money for their next campaign. And many of our most able leaders shy away from public office because they don not have access to large sums of money or don't have a famous name. This actually restricts good qualified people from running.

Americans for Campaign Reform (ACR's) approach offers a complete solution to the problem, not just another ineffective piecemeal reform. And here is the surprise: it is not expensive. For $1.8 billion per year—or Just $6 per citizen – our government can publicly fund all elections for the U.S. Senate, House and the Presidency. Considering over $31 Billion dollars was spent on true pork alone last year this is a drop in the bucket. This is a fraction of the taxpayer money wasted every year on projects that reward special interests and their lobbyists. In fact, in 2005, "pork barrel" projects alone cost every U.S. citizen more than $200. The funds would come out of the federal budget whether from the general fund or from revenue raised specifically to support public funding.

By removing financial resources as a barrier, public funding will expand the field of potential qualified candidates. Values and ideas will stand out, not special interest dollars. Wealthy special interests and their hired lobbyists will no longer have a commanding influence over our politics and government. Instead, elected officials will have more time to communicate with constituents and focus on our country's challenges. Leaders will be accountable to voters, not just large donors. Leaders will have more time to focus on solving problems, rather than raising campaign money. More citizens will participate in the political process. The legislative system will represent all segments of our society.

So it costs us less and eliminates the special interests and domineering corporate influence in one fell swoop and we have taken our country back and insures that we can not fall back into bad habits. Incumbents raise an average of 500% more than their challengers in the current model everyone wants to buy access of the person that is in office eventually leading to corruption, greed, scandal or worse. Fundraising costs for federal campaigns comprise and estimated 20-30% of total campaign contributions public funding greatly reduces this cost. Recruitment of a potential candidate will not focus on a candidate's ability to raise large amounts of campaign funds. This will also free up the elected official to spend more time with his constituents because raising the money to finance a successful campaign frequently consumes over 30-40% of a congressional candidates time, and up to 50% for a Presidential candidate. The future of our country can be shaped by qualified candidates instead of athletes and actors. When you look at our current process one must admit that we do not want to fund candidates with the existing method any longer.

So who does your Congressman work for?

Well he works for us right?! Well, in theory, yes, but only in theory. In reality politicians live and die by campaign contributions it is their life blood; it is all they worry about for 4 years. So if you take a look at who provides campaign contributions in relation to who runs the country then the answer is no, your congressman does not work for you, follow the money.

$2.6 Billion dollars worth of "influence" was purchased in 2006, you can track every dollar at this website below. Sadly once you see the volume of this corruption and it sickens you, you will realize just what a vast charade Congress is. It does not matter who gets into office big industry will make donations and buy them next. Or pay the other side to get them out. Imagine how many "contributions" do not make the list. Take a look here and tell me if you still think you have a say in America.

Top Spenders, 2006

Client	Total
US Chamber of Commerce	$72,740,000
AARP	$23,160,000
General Electric	$20,960,000
American Medical Assn	$19,880,000
AT&T Inc	$19,110,720

US Telecom Assn	$18,380,000
Pharmaceutical Rsrch & Mfrs of America	$18,100,000
American Hospital Assn	$17,435,135
National Assn of Realtors	$16,780,000
Northrop Grumman	$16,769,865
Exxon Mobil	$14,540,000
National Cable & Telecommunications Assn	$14,020,000
Verizon Communications	$13,452,500
Southern Co	$13,300,000
National Assn of Manufacturers	$13,240,000
Alliance of Automobile Manufacturers	$13,028,508
Altria Group	$12,870,000
Pfizer Inc	$11,800,000
Edison Electric Institute	$11,000,000
VeriSign Inc	$10,569,350

http://www.opensecrets.org/politicians/index.asp It is frightening click on any politician

Top Spenders by Industry **Top Industries, 2006**

Industry	Total
Pharmaceuticals/Health Products	$176,323,686
Insurance	$130,326,537
Computers/Internet	$109,296,719
Electric Utilities	$104,460,227
Business Associations	$104,424,677

Education	$88,044,051
Real Estate	$86,847,313
Hospitals/Nursing Homes	$82,113,406
Oil & Gas	$73,173,623
TV/Movies/Music	$71,674,267
Misc Manufacturing & Distributing	$68,661,356
Civil Servants/Public Officials	$68,560,181
Automotive	$66,098,779
Misc Issues	$63,925,129
Securities & Investment	$60,464,217
Telephone Utilities	$60,440,188
Health Professionals	$60,234,429
Air Transport	$56,036,715
Telecom Services & Equipment	$55,618,734
Commercial Banks	$43,328,507

Ranked Sectors, 2006

Sector	Total
Finance, Insurance & Real Estate	$372,510,339
Health	$359,043,610
Misc Business	$338,468,561
Communications/Electronics	$330,267,243
Energy & Natural Resources	$235,381,226

Other	$204,485,257
Transportation	$192,027,901
Ideological/Single-Issue	$127,122,880
Defense	$123,732,813
Agribusiness	$88,870,543
Construction	$38,095,837
Labor	$30,778,883
Lawyers & Lobbyists	$27,989,049

WHERE ARE THE FIGURES FROM?

Lobbyists have to file semi-annual reports with the Secretary of the Senate and the Clerk of the House identifying their clients, the lobbyists working for each client, and the amount of income they receive. Companies have to report their overall lobbying expenditures and the names of any lobbyists employed as part of an in-house lobbying effort. Data are periodically updated to reflect late filings and amendments.

Corporations and special interests are spending almost $3 billion dollars a year on "influence" almost $5,000,000 per candidate, and they own them do you see your name on this list? Tell me who runs the country; what you have always suspected about Washington is completely true and completely changeable. This also represents what was reported how many junkets, under the table payments, expensive dinners, free trips, donations and "gifts" go unreported? About the same amount? More? Why would the drug companies need to spend $172M dollars for influence when you have a medical need their products? Lastly for any purists out there saying, hey, this is our political system at work please sit and ponder on what exactly a $1 million dollar campaign contribution from say, big oil or big banks, or big drug is for? What are they buying? Then of course when it does go too far there are always the wonderful scandals. Hillary Clinton herself was forced to return almost $1 million in campaign contributions from unscrupulous sources and other donations which she received are under investigation. Is this who we the people want having access to our Senators?

$90,000 of "bacon" Found in Congressman's freezer

Bringing home the bacon! $90,000 cash found in his freezer, he will not step down, and he was re-elected! Great job Congressman Jefferson !! This what our tax money is paying for. Rep. William Jefferson, D-La., was indicted Monday on federal charges of racketeering, soliciting bribes and money-laundering in a long-running bribery investigation into business deals he tried to broker in Africa. The indictment handed up in federal court in Alexandria., Va., Monday is 94 pages long and lists 16 alleged violations of federal law that could keep Jefferson in prison for up to 235 years, according to a Justice Department official who has seen the document. Jefferson is accused of soliciting bribes for himself and his family, and also for bribing a Nigerian official. Almost two years ago, in August 2005, investigators raided Jefferson's home in Louisiana and found $90,000 in cash stuffed into a box in his freezer. Jefferson, 63, whose Louisiana district includes New Orleans, has said little about the case publicly but has maintained his innocence. He was re-elected last year despite the looming investigation. Another Jefferson associate, Louisville, Ky., telecommunications executive Vernon Jackson, pleaded guilty to paying between $400,000 and $1 million in bribes to Jefferson in exchange for his assistance securing business deals in Nigeria and other African nations. Jackson was sentenced to more than seven years in prison. http://www.msnbc.msn.com/id/19031423/

Convicted of selling $2.4 million dollars of "influence"

Rep. Randy "Duke" Cunningham said Monday he is resigned from Congress after pleading guilty to taking more than $2 million in bribes in a criminal conspiracy involving at least three defense contractors. After entering his plea in San Diego, California, the eight-term California Republican said he was "deeply sorry." "The truth is I broke the law, concealed my conduct and disgraced my office," he told reporters, his voice strained with emotion. "I know I will forfeit my reputation, my worldly possessions -- most importantly the trust of my friends and family." Asked by U.S. District Judge Larry Burns if he had accepted cash and gifts and then tried to influence the Defense Department on behalf of the donors, Cunningham said, "Yes, your honor." Under the agreement, Cunningham acknowledged a conspiracy to commit bribery, mail and wire fraud and tax evasion. He also pleaded guilty to a separate tax evasion violation for failing to disclose income in 2004.

14 Members of Congress imprisoned in a 5 year span

From 1992 to 1998 more 14 different members of Congress were indicted and imprisoned on criminal charges, most notably Dan Rostenkowski (D-Ill.) Dan Rostenkowski was in Congress for 36 years and the Head of the very powerful House Ways and Means Committee which controlled a vast amount of every single dollar spent by Congress, so no one really knows how much wound up in his pocket since he was overseeing the spending of billions of dollars weekly. Rostenkowski was indicted in 1994 on 17 felony charges, including the embezzlement of $695,000 in taxpayer and campaign funds. The longtime House Ways and Means chairman plea-bargained his way down to two counts of mail fraud and served 17 months in a Wisconsin minimum-security prison. There is too much temptation and no oversight in the current system.

Lessons in Politics
BEIJING — A Beijing court on Tuesday sentenced to death China's former food and drug safety chief for accepting more than $800,000 in bribes from pharmaceutical companies.

Another Chinese government official Zheng Xiaoyu was convicted on charges of taking bribes and dereliction of duty, Xinhua news agency reported, citing the Beijing Municipal No. 1 Intermediate People's Court. China sentenced the former head of the State Food and Drug Administration to death for corruption. In America he would have been run for Senator or for a Sr. cabinet position for taking $800,000 in bribes, he is now ready to step up to the big leagues.

The United States should stand up and take a lesson on how to act when public officials are discovered to be corrupt, manipulative, break the law, and work against the common interest. We should put them to death instead of on the talk show/book-circuit gig for $50,000 a day. These people took an oath to uphold the Constitution of the United States these acts amount to treason, why not punish them for treason.

DESTROYING AMERICA

Chapter 6   Runaway Government Spending and Pork

Pure "pork" projects accounted for $31 Billion dollars in 2006, a total of 9,963 projects were undertaken. I will detail a few of the more notable disasters with some egregious details. Our elected officials approved $31 Billion in known pork projects, so what amount say at least double or triple that amount probably slipped by undetected or was wrapped into something else. So this is $100 Billion dollars that slipped by. The larger problem is the normal course of business in Washington and normal spending committees in Congress. The age old idea of bringing home the bacon is not good for our country. Where because you sit on the highway committee means you get a bigger share of the highway pie even though you have the least populist state Alaska Congressman Don Young was "bringing home" $560 Million dollars for an unneeded highway project, how many extra aircraft carriers, highways, missiles, and buildings slip by each year?

Without a doubt I will detail were some of your money has gone over the last 10 years, there are times where it will not be pretty, none-the-less you bought it. So where is all this government money going and why is the National Debt almost $10 Trillion dollars? Well there is a category of waste with spending so ludicrous that no normal human being would have sanctioned these projects unless they work at the Capital…. then again I did say no normal human being not a US Senator, be forewarned if you read this you will pass from the ridiculous to the sublime.

Yucca Mountain

Some Government Genius decided in the late 1970s that rather than have 100+ nuclear waste storage facilities around the country we should have one central storage area for all of it to "save money" The U.S. Department of Energy began studying Yucca Mountain, Nevada, in 1978 to determine whether it would be suitable for the nation's first long-term geologic repository for spent nuclear fuel and high-level radioactive waste. Currently stored at 126 sites around the nation, these materials are a result of nuclear power generation and national defense programs. Sounds good on paper.....

On July 23, 2002, President Bush signed House Joint Resolution 87, allowing the DOE to take the next step in establishing a safe repository in which to store our nation's nuclear waste. The Department of Energy is currently in the process of preparing an application to obtain the Nuclear Regulatory Commission license to proceed with construction of the repository. Yucca Mountain, located 100 miles northwest of Las Vegas, is the proposed site of a repository to hold the nation's nuclear waste. The U.S. Department of Energy wants to use the mountain to bury 77,000 tons of radioactive waste. Why Yucca? Simple, the US Government owns 74% of the land in Nevada and there aren't enough voters to say no or have an impact to someone's campaign. Politics, Bad Site choice and cost overruns where pointed out from before the start: FROM a 1998 Nevada Government study before the digging began:

" In 1982, Department of Energy (DOE's) initial estimates for characterizing three potential repository sites under the original Nuclear Waste Policy Act was in the neighborhood of $80 million per site. To date, almost $4 billion has been spent on Yucca Mountain alone, with the total cost for simply characterizing - not constructing or operating - a single repository site now estimated at over $5 billion. " ****

Now $8 Billion Dollars just to study the mountain. Oh and the Government wanted a 10,000 year guarantee from the study. " (1998 Memo) In its most recent Total System Life Cycle Cost Assessment for the high-level radioactive waste program in 1995, DOE estimated the overall cost of the program at just over $34.7 billion (in 1996 dollars)." ***(Now over $60 Billion, and not ready until 2017 adding another $50 Billion, for a TOTAL of $110 Billion dollars, not including DOE and NRC fees which will add another $40-$50 Billion to the total)

So thus far, we spent $31 Billion dollars of taxpayer money over 11 years for a hole in the mountain that no one wants to use. (and is not ready for use, and it may not be safe) This does not include DOE payments for onsite storage at existing facilities that will be billed to the Government (you) So instead of a $29 billion taxpayer liability, Congress may well leave the country with a $40 billion or more unfunded obligation if this new and ill-considered legislation should become law. Because the NRC said to the power plants don't move your spent fuel we will store it all for you. $28 Billion more (in 2006 dollars) before it is ready? NRC says it will be ready in 2010, the DOE guy who runs the dept for 30 years says 2017 maybe, what will the costs be by then?

According to the target numbers it will be $110 Billion dollars for a $34.7 Billion dollar project. By the way it is not ready for use and has at least 5 more years of litigation before they can do anything with it, if you look at the web site you would think it was in full operation and they don't mention the cost anywhere. $61 Billion dollars for an unusable hole in the mountain (2007)

This is one truly horrendous example of government spending, but it sheds light on the issue. How many "other" Yucca mountains are there? How many programs under or over a $1 billion dollars fly under the radar completely and are similar disasters? How many other black holes are we funding with our $10 Trillion dollar deficit? And WHY! We spent $8 Billion dollars to study a mountain. 11 years and $31 Billion dollars total thus far for a hole in a mountain that we are not using, that is not ready and is over 200% of the initial cost and may be an ill conceived plan.

Can anyone trust Department of Energy Math? Have they ever been right before?

The estimated cost of DOE's highly touted Supercolliding Super Conductor project in Texas went from $5.9 billion when it was started in the late 1980's to $11 billion - and still rising - when the program was canceled in 1993.

The waste vitrification plant completed at DOE's Savannah River Site in South Carolina was 62% over budget and 6 ½ years behind schedule.

The Fuels and Materials Examination Facility at the Hanford site in Washington was 39% over budget. With a huge corruption issue with Bechtel the contractor.

The DOE also estimated that it might possibly need its own rail system for transportation of the materials to Yucca mountain but it was not necessary, this was estimated at $250 Million dollars and was an optional item. DOE is now upping its request from $1 Billion dollars to $2 Billion dollars for a NEEDED rail system for transportation of the materials to Yucca, no longer optional this expenditure is NOT included as part of the Yucca Mountain project costs. Seems no one wants to haul nuclear waste.

Just to put this in perspective we spent $31 Billion dollars on this so far. If Yucca mountain was a NYSE "company" it would rank in between AT&T, UPS, and Dow Chemical (in GROSS not Net TOTAL SALES in 2005) , positions 40, 42, 44 in the Fortune 500 in 2005.

To say this is a dimension beyond ridiculous is and understatement, but did I ever tell you about the bridge to nowhere... .

So How Much Does a Bridge to "Nowhere" Cost?

A: $320 Million

OK so other than a $61 BILLION Dollar hole in a mountain are there any other egregious acts of spending by the US Government?

Dubbed the "Bridge to Nowhere," the bridge in Alaska would connect the town of Ketchikan (population 8,900) with its airport on the Island of Gravina (population 50) at a cost to federal taxpayers of $320 million, by way of three separate earmarks in the recent highway bill. At present, a ferry service runs to the island, but some in the town complain about its wait (15 to 30 minutes) and fee ($6 per car). The Gravina Island bridge project is an embarrassment to the people of Alaska and the U.S. Congress. Fiscally responsible Members of Congress should be eager to zero out its funding.

Today, Senator Tom Coburn (R-OK) will offer an amendment to the Senate's appropriation bill to transfer the $223 million that Congress had previously approved for a bridge in Ketchikan, Alaska, to fund reconstruction of a hurricane-damaged bridge in Louisiana. (Instead of building a bridge to nowhere)

A $320 Million dollar bridge for a population of 8,900 and it was APPROVED!!!!!
A Christian Science Monitor analysis shows the average lawmaker wins $14 million worth of highway projects, while members of the Senate and House Transportation Committees pull in about $40 million each - some far more. On the House side, Jim Oberstar (D) of Minnesota got $90 million in projects and minority leader Nancy Pelosi of California was awarded $120 million. Speaker Dennis Hastert (R) pulled in $160 million, and Young of

Alaska, the committee chair, lined up $590 million - surpassing many states with 20 times its population. Unrepentant, Young has said he'd "be ashamed of himself" if he hadn't delivered spoils to Alaska, which relies on federal subsidies for its transportation infrastructure.

No highway spending is more controversial than bridge work. Senator McCain points with incredulity to a $200 million earmark being sought by Young for the Knik Arm Bridge (a down payment on a cost that could reach 10 times that much) and to the $175 million Alaska is attempting to secure for the sister project, a span that would connect Ketchikan with Gravina, home to only a few hundred people. One impetus, rarely mentioned, is that the bridge would create an easy route for timber companies to log Pacific rain forest.

"If you look at the Big Dig tunnel project in Boston, which was considered the poster child of embarrassment as far as federal transportation boondoggles," says Ashdown, "it will end up appearing to be a great deal if the Gravina and Knik Arm bridges are built."
The proposed $2 billion Knik Arm Bridge - one of several projects that could make Alaska the biggest winner in this year's transportation-bill sweepstakes - has stirred outrage from critics who see it as pork-barrel spending that will send federal deficits spiraling up. Some call it "the Big Dig of the Far North," a reference to Boston's overbudget tunnel project.

Boston Big Dig
Original Estimate $1.4-$2.6 Billion dollars

When construction began, the project cost, including the Charles River crossing, was estimated at $5.8 billion. Eventual cost overruns were so high that the chairman of the Massachusetts Turnpike Authority, James Kerasiotes, was fired in 2000. His replacement had to commit to an $8.55 billion cap on federal contributions. Total expenses eventually passed $15 billion. Before lawsuits.

This is a total cost of over $4 BILLION DOLLARS PER MILE
Government Waste Part 3
But this is an Isolated case right?? (The first step is awareness)

"According to some estimates we can not track $2.3 trillion dollars in transactions" Donald Rumsfeld Sept 10, 2001 (grew to $3.4 TRILLION)

But "No where" seems to be a popular spot
$700 Million Dollars for the Railroad to No where
Not to be out done by Alaska's bridge to nowhere, Mississippi has there own way to burn your money

Much of this has focused on a $700 million earmark backed by Senators Trent Lott (R-MS) and Thad Cochran (R-MS) for Mississippi's "Railroad to Nowhere." In terms of sheer profligacy, this earmark far exceeds even Alaska's infamous "Bridge to Nowhere." In comparison to the train's $700 million price tab, the $220 proposed for the Alaska bridge is less than a third the price of the Lott/Cochran earmark. And although the bridge's purpose and benefits were questionable, details of the project were clear and fully disclosed, and lawmakers and citizens could judge it on its merits, or lack thereof. So the Bridge to NoWhere is actually a bargain!!!!! At only 1/3 rd the cost maybe we should buy two !!!!

The "Railroad to Nowhere" proposal, in contrast, is anything but clear and straightforward, and contradictory details about its motivation and implementation continue to leak out from Mississippi. Mississippi's senators contend that the proposal is intended to improve rail safety, but as The Washington Post has reported, similar safety issues exist nationwide and "Mississippi's rail-accident rate from 2001 to 2005 reached a 30-year low.

Think there's any waste here?

Consolidating duplicative programs will save money and improve government service. In addition to those programs that should be eliminated completely, Congress should consolidate the following sets of programs:

342 economic development programs;

130 programs serving the disabled;

130 programs serving at-risk youth;

90 early childhood development programs;

75 programs funding international education, cultural, and training exchange activities;

72 federal programs dedicated to assuring safe water;

50 homeless assistance programs;

45 federal agencies conducting federal criminal investigations;

40 separate employment and training programs;

28 rural development programs;

27 teen pregnancy programs;

26 small, extraneous K–12 school grant programs;

23 agencies providing aid to the former Soviet republics;

19 programs fighting substance abuse;

17 rural water and waste-water programs in eight agencies;

17 trade agencies monitoring 400 international trade agreements;

12 food safety agencies;

11 principal statistics agencies; and

Four overlapping land management agencies

Federal Spending has grown at 290% since 1962, median income only by 54%

and the US Population has grown by less than 10% per year avg. so who are they spending this money on? And why is Federal spending growing at 10+X times the rate of population growth + inflation + and CPI ?

Earmarks (PORK) has exploded 2000% from 1991 to 2006

Earmark projects, otherwise known as "pork" projects, have proliferated in recent years. There were more earmarks in 2005 than from 1991 to 1999 combined. Although the number of earmarks went down in 2006, their cost increased $6 billion in one year -- from $23 billion in 2005 to $29 billion in 2006. Many earmarks are not included in the bills, but rather in non-binding conference or committee reports. This is undisputed Pork, not inefficiency or waste but pure pork projects.

Look at the numbers you do not need to be Albert Einstein to understand that this can not continue

Yes it is daunting, nauseating and frustrating, and it is all too easy to throw up your hands and say I can not have any effect on this. Remember this is the stuff we are leaving to our children, they are inheriting $10 Trillion dollars in debt and bridges and trains to nowhere.

So just like a drug or alcohol treatment program the first step here is simply awareness, admit this exists and it is a problem and as a US tax paying citizen I expect some thing to be done to reduce these ridiculous expenditures. Q: Other than this really bad pork are we throwing money away on anything else? A: YES.

$10 Billion "squandered" in Iraq Auditors: Billions squandered in Iraq WASHINGTON - About $10 billion has been squandered by the U.S. government on Iraq reconstruction aid because of contractor overcharges and unsupported expenses, and federal investigators warned Thursday that significantly more taxpayer money is at risk.

The three top auditors overseeing work in Iraq told a House committee their review of $57 billion in Iraq contracts found that Defense and State department officials condoned or allowed repeated work delays, bloated expenses and payments for shoddy work or work never done. $10 Billion waste on $57 Billion is 17.5% If this is any indication of what is happening to the $1 Trillion dollars for Iraq this will really ugly, lets not say we were not warned.

Extra Government Waste Part 2

Why Is $59 Billion Missing From HUD? - United States. Department of Housing and Urban Development But this waste you point out its just isolated cases of trifling amounts isn't it?

$59,000,000,000.00 MISSING. Billions of dollars are missing from the U.S, Department of Housing and Urban Development's books. Some HUD officials blame computer glitches; others allege widespread graft. The Department of Housing and Urban Development (HUD) has earned a failing grade from the House Government Reform subcommittee on Government Management for the way the agency manages taxpayers' money.

Subcommittee chairman Stephen Horn, R-Calif., is said to be furious that HUD's most recent financial report shows the agency is unable to balance its checkbook and cannot account for $59 billion.

For most Americans, it is incomprehensible that $59 billion could be missing from the ledger of a single agency. But despite years of earning failing grades -- as well as years of being unable to account for tens of billions of dollars -- the Clinton/Gore management team at HUD has continued to shell out hundreds of millions of dollars to the same contractors hired to ensure financial systems are in place and working. It doesn't take a certified public accountant to see that HUD Secretary Andrew Cuomo's financial house is not in order, and Susan Gaffney, the inspector general (IG) of HUD, tells Insight, "It's more serious than you know."   There was also a small accounting adjustment in 1998 for $17,000,000,000.00 ($17 Billion dollars missing ooops) as well.

The $100 load of laundry from our friends at Halliburton
While this is some information regarding Halliburton, it is just a matter of time before all government contracts for Iraq have similar or worse findings. As an American and taxpayer, I hope you are concerned that this "War on Terror" does not give any company the right to rip us off without end, while hiding behind our troops, like a bunch of fucking spineless, leeches. After all it is your money. But I want to share some of the things I have just read regarding Halliburton and they are only one of many contractors, who seem concerned with only one thing and its not our troops. Unsupported and over billing in the amount of $1.8 Billion dollars, some egregious examples of "cost plus" contracts, sure does not stop us from awarding them more

contracts, and is competition not the "American Way", have you ever seen a no bid contract? Hey here's some buckets of money, where do you want it?

500 Halliburton Executives staying in the Iraq area who 99.9% of the time do not leave the 5 Star hotel where they stay in Qatar, all have a brand new Suburban's, Navigators, Escalades, with every available option, sunroof, DVD, chrome wheels, the lease on these vehicles is $7000 per month, so besides the fact that they are unused, we are paying $250,000 for vehicles which cost $45,000, I'm not even going to ask if the DVD player and chrome rims are strategic to the war effort. And it's a lease, they don't even own the vehicle. They sub contract whatever they can locally, they received a 5 year garbage hauling contract for $80 Million, the total cost to them is under $900,000 over 5 years not a bad profit.

Halliburton charges $99 per load of laundry per soldier at least weekly; soldiers complain that the clothes come back grimier then prior to washing, more on why they feel grimier below. Soldiers have been told by their CO's that they can not do their own laundry, why? 22 Truckers have sued Halliburton for making them drive convoys up and down the highway in harms way with empty trucks so H can bill for it. They kind of felt getting shot for carrying nothing was not as patriotic as it seems. H was making $1000 per hour per truck, the truckers were paid about $2000 a week, apparently not worth dying for. Halliburton is using brand new Mercedes trucks, each cost $100,000, with no spare parts stocked or carried, for most support operations, and a strict policy that anything that breaks down must be destroyed, so it can not be used by the enemy, a broken gasket or fan belt can cause destruction of a brand new truck. Oil filter = $100,000, BTW this is the "Cost Plus" methodology, who would sign off on a contract where I can bill you whatever I want to? Imagine what "cost plus" would mean for any items in the real world, you are building a house and you're contractor says he did not want the delivery to be late so he just bought a brand new truck to go get a load of gravel, they ran out of the cheaper plyboard so they bought aged mahogany for the sheathing, decided to wire the house with gold instead of copper, and he needed a new H3 to survey the lot.

Halliburton charges the DoD $45 for a 6 pack of Coke or Pepsi, but its not imported its bottled on site royalty free, only cost is the can and the sugar mix, about 10c. I saved the 2 best for last, water purification specialist Ben Carter testified before congress, his job was to provide clean, safe water for the troops for showering, cooking, drinking etc. He tested water at 67 Halliburton water treatment plants and found that 63 were NOT providing safe water. Im not talking hard water or a little dirty when he says not safe he means NOT! Safe, as in it contained Malaria, Typhus, Geosporadi, other extremely dangerous pathogens. Gravely concerned he told Halliburton that he wanted to notify the troops who were using this water daily of the health risks associated and he was warned by his employer that "the people of the military were none of his concern".

H refuses to run a 24 hour buffet for the troops because it makes more money charging per meal, several chow lines and mess hall attacks have been targeted with soldiers killed because of this practice. The government talks a lot of shit, "you're either with us or you're with uncle Benny" , support our troops, our bravest, in harms way, keeping freedom, keeping us safe, and a whole ton of money is spent "on their behalf", in the name of Patriotism, and Democracy, but none of the money seems to actually benefit them or just by coincidence some of it trickles on them.

You can see first hand how much the Government really cares, Walter Reed Hospital is a perfect example, and Rumsfelds "go to war with the Army you have" comment 3 years after the war started. The CEOs of these companies (Halliburton, KBR, Bechtel, CACI, and OTHERS) each made over $40 Million last year, any many millions more in stock options, how much do the kids taking the bullets get paid?

$99 load of laundry, $250,000 lease on a $45,000 vehicle, and deadly water, all paid for by us.

Another Triple Standard
US Government sues Jackson Hewitt Tax preparation firm over $70 Million in fraud. Part of the double-double standard, if a private company screws up they will be held accountable and face criminal charges. But when the Government screws up NO ONE will be held accountable.

FEMA wastes $40 Million of food for Katrina victims, no one will be held accountable.
In all, hundreds of truckloads of food, worth more than $40 million, are being thrown away or scavenged for unspoiled contents to be offered to domestic hunger-relief groups, FEMA officials said. Most of the meals were commercial versions of the military's Meals Ready to Eat, which were ruined despite being engineered to withstand the demands of desert and jungle climates.

20,000+ FEMA Trailers sit never used, others improperly left out uncovered, uncared for.

Some trailers never used FEMA spent $2.7 billion to buy 145,000 mobile homes and trailers after Katrina and Rita hit the Gulf Coast in August and September 2005, paying a bulk-rate price of about $19,000 per trailer, on average. FEMA now has 60,000 trailers in storage nationwide; several thousand of them — exactly how many is not clear — were never used. These trailers are being auctioned off and are killing the new RV market for dealers. AND Yes, we are paying to store them.

Billions squandered in Iraq, no one will face charges

More than one in six dollars charged by U.S. contractors were questionable or unsupported, nearly triple the amount of waste the Government Accountability Office estimated last fall." There is no accountability," said David M. Walker, who heads the auditing arm of Congress. "Organizations charged with overseeing contracts are not held accountable. Contractors are not held accountable. The individuals responsible are not held accountable." 1 in 6 dollars unsupported? How does that play out in relation to $446 BILLION already spent? And another $450 BILLION on the way? And if you owe $1 dollar to the IRS they will be up your ass for it, but if you screw up for a few billion you either qualify for a Senator or Cabinet position.

DESTROYING AMERICA

Chapter 7 - Drugs

The Other War on Drugs

Our next addiction: drugs. While Nancy Reagan helped increase awareness on the War on Drugs with the popularity of the "Just say NO" program, the war on this dreadful "scourge" began back in the Nixon Era. So after over 30 years how successful has the "War on Drugs" been?

One of the first objective measures would be availability and street price. If we look at street price as a measure of effectiveness of the War on Drugs, the street price would have risen based upon an effective effort of keeping drugs out, because less supply drives the prices up. A lower street price would mean high availability. The cost of living has doubled almost 4 times since 1976 (COL roughly doubles every 8 years, for sake of comparison a 1st Class Postage stamp in 1976 was .13c)

In 1976 a dose of a recreational substance (cocaine, heroin) was about $20 and it was analyzed as being 10-20% pure. By comparison the same drugs today (meth, crack, cocaine, heroin, xtc, even more choices!) are $5 a dose and are between 80-90% purity. 5 X Times more potent.

Mathematical Analysis shows:

Drugs are now 600 TIMES LESS EXPENSIVE than when the WAR on DRUGS began

Six Hundred Times LESS 600 X less, easier to get, more potent, and more addicting

We spend $50 Billion+ directly on this "war" yearly and these are the results. (period)

Like the War on Poverty, the War in Vietnam, this is yet another war we are "losing", I hope we never declare "war" on education because that would surely have the same results. I think after 30 years it is long overdue for a reality check and a smarter approach.

I am not faulting those who put their lives in harms way. If this war has been going on for 30 years I guess we are not fighting this war very intelligently. Case in point the Agencies arrest the lowest level players in the trade it has no effect, but it does fill up jail cells. And they trade one lowlife for another lowlife's testimony, we have 100,000 paid informants on our payroll, they do not file a W-2 or a 1040 either. A vicious cycle of lies and deceit, paid for by you.

Second, since the early 1960s and the Corona spy satellite program we have had the capability to have surveillance on any part of the globe, at the height of the Cold War we knew whether or not Russia had a missile silo door open, with a resolution of one square meter. Today's technology has 10 times that capability. Are acres of crops growing that hard to spot? Are they put into invisible boats and planes? Are we just not fighting this correctly? Or is it something else entirely? The banks sure do not mind getting the overnight funds rate and interest on the cash deposits of over $1 Trillion dollars per year, it seems that the banks would know where large cash deposits are coming from but somehow the government doesn't.

The Real Cost of Drugs

.... so what is the street price? That I don't know but I know what it costs you!

How much do drugs cost? Well that depends,

If you are caught, it costs the taxpayer $400,000 per dosage + the Human Cost

What! How?

What the government does not point out is that anyone arrested who can not afford a top notch lawyer and gets convicted (spelled p-o-o-r) for an illegal amount of drugs (recreational, personal use, not pounds) spends a mandatory 10 years in jail. This is longer than a rapist will get after good behavior. It costs $40,000 per YEAR per Inmate to house a criminal (you can look it up) So the cost to you for one of these bad, bad people is $400,000 minimum (10 years Mandatory part of Just Say No)

There are over 2.5 million people in Jail, over 75%-80% are "drug related" charges, (possession)

"The latest numbers are out: nearly 800,000 Americans were arrested on marijuana charges in 2005. " "American taxpayers are now spending more than a billion dollars per year to incarcerate its citizens for pot. That's according to statistics recently released by the U.S. Department of Justice's Bureau of Justice Statistics." Imagine the costs involved in processing 1 million people for this.

BUT prior to 1986 these amounts of drugs were not considered "Felony" conditions so there was no prison population explosion. The Police do not always catch the right people, and because of the techniques the Police use and the deals they make the real criminals walk, leaving others on the hook. It's about quantity not quality. More arrests mean more manpower and bigger budgets!

Cops don't arrest murderers before they kill or burglars before they strike or stop Jeffrey Dahmer they arrest people with drugs it's a lot easier and they get to confiscate their cars and property. Everything confiscated can be sold off to add additional forces to the War on drugs! 1 in 3 of those arrested winds up back in jail, half of those for life, and the human cost is far higher. Ex-Cons are also very popular in the job market.

Private companies like Wacknehut and CCC are making fortunes out of the business of destroying human lives, legally.

For a first time offender: Wouldn't re-hab, education, counseling and mandatory drug testing be a much smarter solution? And far less costly, both monetarily and in human costs? Again we have $40,000 a year to hide a mistake but none to fix it? Is this really how we want to continue living? We have the highest percentage of people in prison of ALL civilized nations including Russia, US is over 5% and growing, is this what we should be spending money on? This isn't about getting "soft" on crime this is about common sense and morality and the first step is awareness. The current human cost far outweighs the economic ones. Drug addiction is a medical problem not a criminal one.

I am not in any way shape or form condoning drug usage. Other civilized nations do not do what we do. The way in which the US has been dealing with this problem is not effective and the costs are far too high. Housing somehow for ten years and giving them no training or skills other than how to be a career criminal is only increasing the success rate of return visits, which seems to be the goal.

BIG PHARMA, Big Drug
The real war on drugs
Welcome to the future.

So how is the Government going pay for all this stuff? That answer is simple: taxes, taxes and taxes upon taxes of taxes. Surcharges, usages fees, excise fees, they will find new names for taxes. Internet tax, email tax, computer tax, broadband tax, Gas, ethanol, property, VAT, national sales tax, EMT, AMT, a tax on the tax on the surcharge, you name it, it will be taxed, and its coming. Along with an RFID National ID card, and bar coded money. As always it will be little insignificant amounts in the beginning but they will never go away and never decrease. Like the rural electric act tax, Universal surcharge on phones, cell phones, cable TV, taxes on gasoline, liquor tax, sales tax etc, etc, etc. So how do you do this and get away with it? Simple, I need you to become a hazed over pill popping zombie, so you don't ask me too many questions. Who else wants that? The Pharmaceutical companies and they are betting $10B a year that you will be!

Prescription drugs are the new cigarettes with even more added danger and side effects!

We have all seen the ads for Roezern with Abe Lincoln, and a

Gopher, and the little butterfly for the sleep aid Lunestra, and the nasty creature living inside you on the Lamisil ads. There are cute little cartoon characters in all of these ads, why? because they are aimed at our kids not at us. The Pharmaceutical companies want them conditioned daily so by the time they reach adulthood they will not think twice about popping pills, pills to sleep, pills to wake up, pills to feel happy, pills to get trim, pills for anxiety, pills for not feeling enough anxiety, pills to get an erection, pills to shrink it down. They just want the endless revenue stream from making you a (legal) drug addict. And our generation has a little more resistance to being over-medicated. Our kids will not have this stigma it is being worn away with $9 Billion dollars of advertising each year. It is a new age version of cigarettes, and 100 times more profitable.

American medicine does not want to find a cure for any ailment. Treat the symptoms and make the patient a cash cow. There is no money in curing you, but there is an endless source of money from treating you monthly. The drug companies are the number 4 industry in terms of total advertising spending. So why are they competing with Ford, Target, Mastercard? Why do you think they are competing for your attention at the same rate as Car commercials, Retail store commercials, and financial services commercials? Why else would people selling drugs compete with this amount of ad spending? To benefit mankind? Logic would dictate: Everyone drives a car, everyone buys stuff at retail stores, everyone banks and uses credit cards, ...Everyone Needs Drugs!!! Everyone Needs Drugs!!! Everyone needs Drugs!!!

Don't think Advertising works? Think that you are too smart for this? "Increases in the sales of the 50 drugs that were most heavily advertised to consumers accounted for almost half the $20.8 billion increase in drug spending last year, according to the study. The remainder of the spending increase came from 9,850 prescription medicines that companies did not advertise or advertised very little. " Heartburn medicine Prilosec was $140 a pop as a prescription; it is now OTC and sells for $18 do you think the $140 price point was a little high? Your co-pay may only be $5 but somebody (you via skyrocketing healthcare costs) made up the difference, that's part of the reason why health care costs are soaring. By the way the same Pharma co. also makes the top competing product to Prilosec. Ask your doctor if its time for Viagra?

The ads will be inside of video games, IPods, instant messengers, cell phones, they want to build a strong base, and they have the money to do it. While heart and cholesterol medication are vital to some people and not imagined illnesses, many of the ads and the way they are presented are definitely suspect and not required for your health.

Do you sometimes feel anxiety? Have trouble sleeping? Trouble waking up? DUH?

Are these all real illnesses?, or just something you can take a pill for?

Why else would they spend $10 BILLION dollars to tell you how much you "need" something, ask your doctor....... (he gets a kickback too BTW) (Measured Media Only) Pharmaceutical brands posted a 41.2% increase in measured ad spending for the first half of 2006, to $1.54 billion, according to TNS Media Intelligence data aggregated by Advertising Age.

The Real War on Drugs
Pharmaceutical companies want to try to increase their number of addicts

Fact: 68% of Children in Foster Care (under care given by the state) are under taking some form of mental illness/problem medication. But less than 15% of children in public schools are under these medications.

Large pharmaceutical companies feel they can increase that number of children from 15% to over 55%, they designed an "initiative" for random mandatory mental health screenings twice a year per child at schools. And sent Congress to delivery the "No-child-left-without-drugs" bill
He did not smile give him drugs, she did not cry give her drugs.......you all need drugs.

Read this in it's entirety because your child could be next. President Bush sold the children from the state of Texas to Eli Lilly for a $764,000 donation your children might sell for less.

Bush plans to screen whole US population for mental illness (Screen = give drugs) British Medical Journal June 21 2004 (Not exactly the National Enquirer as a source) A sweeping mental health initiative will be unveiled by President George W Bush in July. The plan promises to integrate mentally ill patients fully into the community by providing "services in the community, rather than institutions," according to a March 2004 progress report entitled New Freedom Initiative (www.whitehouse.gov/infocus/newfreedom/toc-2004.html). While some praise the plan's goals, others say it protects the profits of drug companies at the expense of the public. Bush established the New Freedom Commission on Mental Health in April 2002 to conduct a "comprehensive study of the United States mental health service delivery system." The commission issued its recommendations in July 2003. Bush instructed more than 25 federal agencies to develop an implementation plan based on those recommendations.

The president's commission found that "despite their prevalence, mental disorders often go undiagnosed" and recommended comprehensive mental health screening for "consumers of all ages," including preschool children. According to the commission, "Each year, young children are expelled from preschools and childcare facilities for severely disruptive behaviors and emotional disorders." Schools wrote the commission, are in a "key position" to screen the 52 million students and 6 million adults who work at the schools.

The commission also recommended "Linkage [of screening] with treatment and supports" including "state-of-the-art treatments" using "specific medications for specific conditions." The commission commended the

Texas Medication Algorithm Project (TMAP) as a "model" medication treatment plan that "illustrates an evidence-based practice that results in better consumer outcomes." Dr Darrel Regier, director of research at the American Psychiatric Association (APA), lauded the president's initiative and the Texas project model saying, "What's nice about TMAP is that this is a logical plan based on efficacy data from clinical trials." He said the association has called for increased funding for implementation of the overall plan. But the Texas project, which promotes the use of newer, more expensive antidepressants and antipsychotic drugs, sparked off controversy when Allen Jones, an employee of the Pennsylvania Office of the Inspector General, revealed that key officials with influence over the medication plan in his state received money and perks from drug companies with a stake in the medication algorithm (15 May, p1153). He was sacked this week for speaking to the BMJ and the New York Times. The Texas project started in 1995 as an alliance of individuals from the pharmaceutical industry, the University of Texas, and the mental health and corrections systems of Texas. The project was funded by a Robert Wood Johnson grant—and by several drug companies. Mr. Jones told the BMJ that the same "political/pharmaceutical alliance" that generated the Texas project was behind the recommendations of the New Freedom Commission, which, according to his whistleblower report, were "poised to consolidate the TMAP effort into a comprehensive national policy to treat mental illness with expensive, patented medications of questionable benefit and deadly side effects, and to force private insurers to pick up more of the tab" .

Larry D Sasich, research associate with Public Citizen in Washington, DC, told the BMJ that studies in both the United States and Great Britain suggest that "using the older drugs first makes sense. There's nothing in the labeling of the newer atypical antipsychotic drugs that suggests they are superior in efficacy to haloperidol [an older "typical" antipsychotic]. There has to be an enormous amount of unnecessary expenditures for the newer drugs."

Olanzapine (trade name Zyprexa), one of the atypical antipsychotic drugs recommended as a first line drug in the Texas algorithm, grossed $4.28bn (£2.35bn; 3.56bn) worldwide in 2003 and is Eli Lilly's top selling drug. A 2003 New York Times article by Gardiner Harris reported that 70% of olanzapine sales are paid for by government agencies, such as Medicare and Medicaid. Eli Lilly, manufacturer of olanzapine, has multiple ties to the Bush administration. George Bush Sr was a member of Lilly's board of directors and Bush Jr appointed Lilly's chief executive officer, Sidney Taurel, to a seat on the Homeland Security Council. Lilly made $1.6m in political contributions in 2000—82% of which went to Bush and the Republican Party. Jones points out that the companies that helped to start up the Texas project have been, and still are, big contributors to the election funds of George W Bush. In addition, some members of the New Freedom Commission have served on advisory boards for these same companies, while others have direct ties to the Texas Medication Algorithm Project.

Bush was the governor of Texas during the development of the Texas project, and, during his 2000 presidential campaign, he boasted of his support for the project and the fact that the legislation he passed expanded Medicaid coverage of psychotropic drugs. Bush is the clear front runner when it comes to drug company contributions. According to the Center for Responsive Politics (CRP), manufacturers of drugs and health products have contributed $764,274 to the 2004 Bush campaign through their political action committees and employees—far outstripping the $149 400 given to his chief rival, John Kerry, by 26 April. Drug companies have fared exceedingly well under the Bush administration, according to the centre's spokesperson, Steven Weiss.

The commission's recommendation for increased screening has also been questioned. Robert Whitaker, journalist and author of Mad in America, says that while increased screening "may seem defensible," it could also be seen as "fishing for customers," and that exorbitant spending on new drugs "robs from other forms of care such as job training and shelter programmes." But Dr Graham Emslie, who helped develop the Texas project, defends screening: "There are good data showing that if you identify kids at an earlier age who are aggressive, you can intervene... and change their trajectory."

And the parents were not exactly elated at this program. 5200 people from all over the country and even from other countries have signed up to oppose President Bush's New Freedom Commission's plan to screen every child in United States schools for "mental illness." These citizens have joined together in the following statement: "We, the undersigned, solemnly declare that we will not allow our children to be the subjects of any form of implementation of New Freedom Commission recommendations to screen our children for signs of 'mental illness.'"

(PRWEB) October 21, 2004 -- A Declaration of Refusal Over 5000 people from all over the country and even from other countries have now signed up to oppose the President Bush's New Freedom Commission's plan to screen every child in United States schools for "mental illness," and get as many as possible on expensive, dangerous psychiatric drugs, in order to profit some of the primary contributors to his presidential campaign.

John Breeding, PhD, director of Texans for Safe Education a citizens group which sponsors the Declaration of refusal along with Parents for a Label and Drug Free Education, states that "Far more people are upset with the President for this plan than his margin of victory in Florida which gave him the election in 2000. I have rarely seen such a bipartisan outpouring of dissent. Parents everywhere are drawing the A Series of articles by Jeanne Lenzer in the British Medical Journal are exposing the corruption behind the Texas Medication Algorithm Project (TMAP), revealing that drug company money played a major role in TMAP development, which subsequently resulted in huge payoffs for their high dollar psychiatric drugs.
Where is the mainstream media? Where is the fair and balanced coverage?

In this line of work, Business is Good
The Dot Coms bombed, Techs went bust, Real estate's bubble is deflating: What is the best line of business to be in, for CA? Can you say Lifetime Monopoly? The Governor of CA made arrangements to ease the overcrowding of the CA prisons. But the CA court system, allows 2 individuals to have power over 30 million residents. The CA prisons because of overcrowding are putting 175,000 people in the space built for 100,000. (how do you do that?) Instead of praising the Governor for making arrangements to house some of California's prison population in other states they stop him and file legal action against him. Rather than ease the strain of the over crowding situation, the courts blocked him, and release prisoners (with time left) every day just to make room. Hmmmnn...... I wonder why?

Do you ask, as I did, why would they want to block our prisoners for being housed in another state? Seems humane, cost effective and the "right" thing to do.........

.....Even worse are private prison operating companies such as Corrections Corporation of America and Wackenhut Corporation. These businesses contract with governments to manage prisons, literally making a profit every time another person is sent to jail. And as the prison population in their hands increases, the influence of the prison operators grows. Increasingly, these companies are offering privatized design, construction, and financing packages to government bodies, and consistently removing the opportunity for public oversight. Accountability for prison conditions under privatization is also greatly reduced, as private prison operators have been essentially granted immunity from federal prosecution.

Socialism
1. a theory or system of social organization that advocates the vesting of the ownership and control of the means of production and distribution, of capital, land, etc., in the community as a whole.
2. procedure or practice in accordance with this theory.

Like...... A large percentage of people being employed by the Government........like if they were say building and managing prisons.
3. (in Marxist theory) the stage following capitalism in the transition of a society to communism, characterized by the imperfect implementation of collectivist principles.

Does spending more on prisons than on education sound like something you would to stand up for and endorse? is this something to aspire to? $7 Billion+/yr to hide our mistakes, but none to prevent them?

Over the past twenty years, the prison population of the United States has grown seven-fold (700%), even though our total population has increased only 20% and our crime rate has decreased. With our total imprisoned population now over 2,500,000, we incarcerate more people per capita than any other country that publishes statistics on prisons, even Russia. The state of California alone has built 20 new prisons since 1980, with other states and the Federal government following suit. Well, we must have "needed them"….. BTW we are only 6% of the worlds population but have 25% of the worlds prison population.

In summary, the expense of prison operations has the paradoxical effect of creating large groups with a vested interest in expanding the prison system even further. Many scholars of the field term this group the "prison-industrial complex," operating, as it does, with public funds but without public oversight, much like the military-industrial complex. Hey wait we all need a $400 hammer.

Lock up is my business, and business is good! $40,000 per person/yr $40x175K=$ 7 B/yr

(According to my math that's $110 per person per day, they could stay at Motel 6 with the free breakfast buffet and we'd save hundreds of millions, even billions of dollars each year)

So if you go and lock up a couple thousand of Wackenhuts prisoners, I mean

California's prisoners, in another state where there is capacity you will be short changing the "managing company fees" by $40,000 per head. And eliminating the need to build another huge $500 million prison this year, needing a full staff of guards, etc. So you leave those guys right where they are.

Fascism

1. (sometimes initial capital letter) a governmental system led by a dictator having complete power, forcibly suppressing opposition and criticism, regimenting all industry, commerce, etc., and emphasizing an aggressive nationalism and often racism.

Communism (see description 2 for possible explanation of CA Corrections system)

1. a theory or system of social organization based on the holding of all property in common, actual ownership being ascribed to the community as a whole or to the state.

2. (often initial capital letter) a system of social organization in which all economic and social activity is controlled by a totalitarian state dominated by a single and self-perpetuating political party.

3. (initial capital letter) the principles and practices of the Communist party.

Capitalism

an economic system in which investment in and ownership of the means of production, distribution, and exchange of wealth is made and maintained chiefly by private individuals or corporations, esp. as contrasted to cooperatively or state-owned means of wealth.

I've included the definitions for sake of clarity, to see what economic model the P-I Industrial complex falls under which economic model?

Gray Davis stayed in power as Governor for a long time primarily for one reason: In California prison guard unions were the number one contributor to the election campaigns of former governor Gray Davis, under whom California's spending on prisons increased by hundreds of millions of dollars per year. They all voted for him, he paid billions of dollars for shiny new prisons to be built and staffed Prison guard unions are notorious for lobbying for tougher sentencing laws, new prison projects, and higher wages. This creates a dangerous positive feedback as each prison expansion increases their membership and influence. The machine is on auto-pilot just keep feeding it money, money, money, your money.

Does this look like a self perpetuating government institution, out of reach of criticism and oversight, completely out of control and growing at a rate exceeding any form of rationale in the "normal" economy. See all this spending is able to be hidden under the banner of "making you safer", "law enforcement", hey you're not getting "soft on crime" are you?, etc so any amount spent is a good amount, except for the suckers footing the bill. I mean you're not a commie are you? Evidently I'm not a commie under the above definitions or is it just good business.   Feel socialized yet?   Take a bite out of crime!

Arnold breaking the law again!!
If you are the Government why do something intelligent when you can do something completely asinine. We can not put the over crowded prisoners in CA where there is room for them, we must build several more $900 million dollar prisons and staff them up with guards. "SACRAMENTO, Calif. -

California's troubled prison system was dealt a setback Tuesday when a judge ruled the state cannot ease its severe overcrowding by transferring inmates elsewhere.

The governor invoked emergency powers in October when he ordered the Corrections Department to send thousands of inmates to private prisons in other states. Two employee unions, including the one representing guards, filed lawsuits alleging the order violated state law.

"Today's disappointing ruling is a threat to public safety," Schwarzenegger said in a statement. "I will not release dangerous criminals to relieve overcrowding. The transfer of inmates is imperative to relieve the pressure on our overburdened prison system." Schwarzenegger's move also violated a ban in the California Constitution on using private companies for jobs usually performed by state workers, the judge ruled. California's 33 state prisons were designed for roughly 100,000 inmates but now hold about 172,000, and a federal judge has given the state until June to reduce overcrowding. To fight overcrowding, Schwarzenegger also has asked lawmakers to review sentencing laws and consider an $11 billion prison and jail building program"

The Judge said no because he knows it means that CA must spend more money to increase the size of California's government by building more jails and hiring more guards and he is a government employee. Do you think the answer is to spend another $11 Billion dollars to house them? This makes military spending seem sane, smart and humane. 75% of these "prisoners" are locked away for drug related offenses why spend Billions of dollars on NON-dangerous, non-violent "criminals". We can get a better group rate at the MOTEL 6 than $40,000/person/year (versus the current $110 /day) $39 bucks including meals!! Arnold this is government stop thinking and trying to do something that makes sense, they'll arrest you.

DESTROYING AMERICA

Chapter 8 - Education – Every Child Left Behind

Our education system is badly broken a majority of educators have known this for a number of years now. The Bush administration thinks that by using a clever slogan that the problem will somehow magically be solved, but a slogan will not fix the problem, only insult us. It may sound cliché because the phrase is overused but in this case it is accurate: our children really are our future, and we are doing the students, our families, the country and our future a disservice by running an education system that does not work. A school system that puts out a sub-par product a student which is prepared for nothing in the real world and compares poorly to their peers in other civilized nations. This is a very complex issue with no easy answer, but business-as-usual on this subject will wind up killing our country and our future.

At first glance one might take the typical American stand of throwing more money at the problem and the problem will go away. In the year 2000 an average of $7,000 was spent annually per student in the school system by 2007 this amount had increased to over $10,000 per student, while in the best case scenario test and aptitude scores stagnated, remained the same and in some cased actually declined. A 50% increase in spending produced very little to no results, so obviously throwing money at the problem is not the answer. Even with the cooked statistics from the Department of Education they can not hide the embarrassing truth, imagine what the unmassaged results would show, if stagnation is the best result they can articulate. Let me define my position on this: spending more and more money to maintain mediocre results and which place our students in the bottom 20% of students in the world is failure. Anyone that would regard this situation as not being left behind should look at the facts.

If money is not the problem then this opens up Pandora's Box. When the stock answer of "more money" is not the problem this opens up the school system to scrutiny and evaluation, and the monolithic, bureaucratic, dictatorship of an organization is entirely averse to anything that would threaten their power and their budget. Moreover any changes would be an admission of problems that school systems have been hiding for years that they are not educating well, and the systems are only passing a certain amount of students through standardized tests the only goal, which is to get funding. Learning anything or getting an actual education in the process is incidental and not really part of the mission of the school. While this may sound insane ask any educator is this is an accurate description of the American education system, and 75% will agree with this statement. Our first problem is American pride, not identifying a problem when it is staring you in the face. America is currently ranked in the bottom quartile of the top 25 industrialized nations in education. Our students can not even place in the 50th percentile versus their German and Belgian and European counterparts in the same grade levels.

The students are not fooled by the system, the following statement is from Kareem Elnahal the Valedictorian of Mainland High School, Mainland High School of New Jersey was Ranked 403rd out of 1,200 schools in Newsweek Magazines "America's Best High Schools" report from August 2005. "The education we have received here is not only incomplete, it is entirely hollow." "It is a grade for the sake of a grade, work for the sake of work." "The spirit of intellectual thought is lost, I know how highly this community values learning, and I urge you to re-evaluate what is means to be educated." An overwhelming majority of the students from Mainland High School agreed with his statements. (CNS News.com, Kate Monaghan June 29, 2006) The superintendent of the school system of course went on to defend the quality of education at Mainland HS, throwing out the key buzzwords of "rank", "blue ribbon" and "top high schools", but for him it's a paycheck he is not going to admit that the valedictorian was right. The Superintendent also pointed out that the education that Elnahal received is permitting him to go to Princeton University. What the Superintendent is even failing to understand is that Elnahal is going to Princeton to spite the hollow education he received not because of the hollow education they provided. He succeeded in spite of the system and Elnahal is the exception not the rule.

From a student perspective there is only one speed or pace of teaching which is set by the teacher so either the student is bored and under challenged, or confused and far behind. The brightest child will be the one left the furthest behind in our current system. Students say school is boring and useless. The teacher will set the pace to very slow to try to keep as many students in the learning process as possible, the "least common denominator" principle. So mathematically at least 50% will find this pace too slow. If the students are learning disjointed trivia and facts, nothing of value, nothing tangible each day why would they want to stay in school? And if you were forced to do this all day long all year long unchallenged and bored or behind and not understanding wouldn't you begin to disconnect from it, or not be engaged by it. As a student how would you begin to feel about your teachers and your parents for making you do this every day. Asking the proverbial so what did you learn in school today? And getting an answer of "nothing" is actually accurate. And this answer is partially correct; because the goal is to pass you through the grade not actually teach you anything. The only mission statement seems to be one of "graduate".

From a teachers perspective, teachers look at their cheating, noisy, IPod wearing, cell phone carrying, unmotivated classes with occasional deadly violence mixed in and wonder why they signed up for this. Teachers often get new additions to the curriculum with very little prior notice and they are expected to be experts instantly on material they have never see before. Teachers also often receive no new resources or money with which to purchase or support the new curriculum. They are also expected to teach multiple subjects and have subject mastery in all of them when certainly it stands to reason that a teacher maybe superb in one or more areas but not as good in another. Teachers have less control in the classroom because there is little they can resort to in terms of discipline. When teachers discipline students they feel they are at risk from parents who disagree with whatever method of discipline that the teacher chose. Discipline can put the teacher at greater risk that the student being disciplined. In this environment the behavior of one child can disrupt the learning of 30 others. Then to spite the teachers' best intentions he or she will be expected to follow school policy written or unwritten of passing X% and failing Y% regardless of his/her observations of the students. All that is important is the classrooms average. Throw in abuse from students, concealed weapons, drugs, maybe even threats or violence and this will round the picture of what the teachers see. A widget on the production line.

American children spend in excess of 20,000 hours attending school from the time they enter elementary school through the time they graduate high school some 12 years later. There is a great deal of research which suggests that up to 80% of everything taught in public education consists of rote memorization which is the ability to memorize desired answers to predictable questions and parrot information. 90% of this information will be stored in the students memory until the test is over and quickly forgotten, having no relevance for the student. Less than 10-15% of learning is devoted to actual "problem solving " these are subjects like solving an algebra problem, building a doghouse, computer programming. Students learn rules, and apply those rules to achieve certain desired results. The 3 categories of behavior to which less than 10% of the instructional effort is devoted to comprise the sought after attribute we call critical thinking. This would be analysis, synthesis and evaluation. Analysis: separating material or concepts into component parts so that an organizational structure can be understood. Synthesis: builds a structure or pattern from diverse elements, putting parts together to form a whole. Evaluation: make judgments about the value of ideas or materials. These skills are essential in the real world and the business world but seldom ever part of the public school curriculum. This where other countries are far ahead of our methods, they spend more time teaching their students how to think and less time on memorizing trivia. Knowing "the when" the year that Caesar crossed the Rubicon is not as important as knowing "the why" why he crossed the Rubicon, which is important, but the date is what makes the test, the when will be on the test, trivia vs. understanding history. Same with the dates for the Declaration of Independence and the Magna Carta and dozens of others, the date is almost irrelevant compared to what the document signifies. A vicious cycle of not teaching substance, not reporting substance in the media, an not requiring substance from our elected officials.

Tests are currently instituted by schools only to serve as a form of punishment and tests have no real other purpose within the school. Tests are issued to compare one student's progress with others in a given area of study. Within classrooms tests are issued to give each student a grade. But the test serves only to indicate which student has a better ability to parrot the desired answers to predictable questions it does not indicate the students understanding of the subject, or if the student learned anything. These tests which test memorization ability are then used to rate the children against each other. Tests do not aid the student they only aid the teacher in providing a grade. To make matters worse some schools grade on a curve where a certain percentage of children regardless of their actual performance will pass the test and other students will fail the test. If tests were really used to evaluate what a student learned or did not learn in an area of study, then the results of the test would be used to target which materials should be re-studied by the student so they could arrive at 100% comprehension of the materials studied, then tests would have a positive role in education. With the amount of technology available giving the student extra study materials to help on what was missed would be a relatively easy matter. If the mission of a school is to teach why wouldn't the school target what was missed and help the student? The specific questions missed are rarely the target for the students review and as in most schools systems there is no time to go back and learn what you missed we have to move on to the next subject. Tests are not used to teach and they need to changed to help educate not simply be punitive.

There is yet another side of these tests and the standardized testing methods. The educational systems reliance upon standardized testing reduces the amount of actual learning that takes place in schools. Teachers are forced to teach students only the information that will be on the tests because of the importance of the tests in determining school funding and student aptitude. Students are well aware of the side effects of standardized testing, where a good portion of the year is spent in preparation for and stressing out over "the test". Students have commented that "a lot of teachers feel pressure to teach us what is going to be on the city and state tests, not what will really connect with us and help us learn." Psychologist and Education Expert Carl Rogers says that this teaching method eliminates the learner's personal discovery of meaning and experience, and lessens the learning process. A large amount of research indicates that standardized testing is one of the leading factors why the traditional education system is ineffective. Psychologist Abraham Maslow has regarded that "the present school system is an extremely effective instrument for crushing peak experiences and forbidding their possibility". How many times have you seen a ridiculous question that will be on one of those standardized tests that you will never see again anywhere else in any facet of your life?

And the students are not immune from this "teaching to the test" phenomenon which exacerbated a new reaction as a response to this environment in the form of "get a degree and get out". The education system and standardized tests do not intrinsically value learning on its own but are only concerned with external motivators. The system creates an environment where most students in school are not there to learn but to complete it and get a degree. This falls in place with the lack of a mission statement. This is not the fault of the student but the result of the value system and structure imposed on the student by the system. The student realizes that they are a widget on the production line, and the school wants the "completed" stamp issued to the student to submit for next years budget. David Larabee makes a convincing argument in his aptly tiled How to Succeed in School Without Really Learning Anything. He says "students are thinking of education as primarily a way to get ahead and therefore the point of seeking an education is to gain a comparative advantage over other people by acquiring a badge- an educational credential'. The educational system demonstrates to the student that learning itself really is not important nor self improvement only what is on the test is important. This makes it difficult for the maturing student to instill personal value and connect with subject matter. It can also be argued that the tests are not effective and that they come at the expense of learning which make actually make the student become disinterested in learning for learning's sake.

Despite great strides and advances in technology, science, medicine, software and electronics our current school system shows very little progress from the students of 40 years ago. Billions and billions of dollars, ($500 Billion in 2006) technology, video, the Internet, and thousands of people have been thrown at this challenge with little to no progress. $10,000 per student in 2007. It is therefore logical to conclude that the existing school system in the form that it is, is intractable, not working or actually failing, (let's face it more money to tread water is failure) and so in need of overhaul that any of the former process improvements de facto had no effect on the system. It is an intransigent, archaic, bureaucratic institution crushed under its own weight which spends more money measuring its horrible performance than it does in educating our students. The education system has been given ample time and money to fix its problems and the United

States is now falling far behind other countries in education and in being able to provide skilled labor for knowledge worker positions. The schools do not work, they are expensive and unproductive, children are dropped through the cracks by the million, and most of the ones that do fall through will never be counted on any government statistic.

When a student fails a test and gets an "F" grade, why aren't the school and the teacher given an "F" as well? They are paid to educate the student and they failed. If you fail at your job you are penalized, why aren't the school systems? The fact that every student does not learn and understand every portion of the material and that students receive poor grades indicates an overwhelming failure of the education system.

Teachers and schools must come to terms with their culpability in this matter. If a student fails, then they have all failed, the student, the teacher, the school and the school system have failed. In education there is a living person future at stake. And these failures have a higher social cost later. School systems are also quick to eliminate "problem" children so that they do not bring the schools grade average down, rather than educate they make many marginal children simply someone else's problem, and surely there will be no statistics on them.

You need to see some of the abysmal statistics of the educational system rather than just the ones shown by the Department of Education, an organization whose entire purpose is to make itself look as good as possible while failing miserably. The school system refers to a high school where no more than 60 percent of the students who start as freshmen make it to their senior year as a "Dropout Factory". That description fits more than one in 10 high schools across America. Associated Press October 29, 2007. Let us look at one of their Department of Educations statistics first, in 1991 the average SAT critical reading result for all students was a score of 499. Now after almost tripling the money spent per child and applying 15 additional years of experience in education and the ability to transfer knowledge to students in the year 2004 the SAT average score was 508, the students tested 8 points higher which is less than a 2% improvement. By the way this average was 503 in 2005 which statistically is zero improvement. The average SAT math score improved from 500 to 518 over the same 15 years so there is no success story there either. We spent 300% more money for a 3% improvement. They will cherry pick one stat that makes them look good and ignore the other 98%. A study released by the Chicago Tribune April 21, 2006 detailed that out of every 100 High School freshman only 6 students would go on to complete a college degree. Chicago is not a rural, farm area, the area is pretty savvy, good metro areas, centrally located, replete with job opportunities the fact that only 6 students out of 100 will continue on in school to earn a degree is surprising. Part of this is because of children getting turned off to education because of the system, after surviving 12 years of boredom, why would you want to sign up and pay for another 4 years? You can rest assured that more than 6% of the jobs in the Chicago metro area require a college degree. In 2006 the drop out rate in the Los Angeles Unified School District was over 50%, half the children in L.A. one of the biggest cities in our nation, do not graduate high school. And surprisingly this is not the highest drop out rate for a school in our country. What else does this tell you? It says that 20-50% of the problems fall right off the radar, and the schools averages still do not improve. To say nothing of the drop outs who are left behind, despite the cool name of the Presidents slogan.

In addition to the education systems abhorrent results, schools are failing to address the changes in American society. School is meant to prepare people to join the workforce. But our national workforce requirements have radically changed from a workforce largely comprised of those who perform physical labor, work in factories, or manufacturing etc, to a service economy which requires knowledge workers who can easily use a computer. 1990 marked the date when there was a shift in our GDP from being a predominantly a manufacturing economy to being a service economy and the work force must follow these trends. We are going to need more than a 6% college graduate rate. Employers are seeking motivated, productive people who can make decisions, have good judgment and have critical thinking skills, employers are looking for people with abilities that are not taught in our schools. In short they are looking for employees who have not been educated by our school system; most of us in the private sector would not consider this a good thing.

The educational system of the United States has not kept up with the various changes in the world it has not even kept up with the changes in America. The American education system must raise its standards because students need more advanced skills than ever to compete in the global world. And the system needs to work smarter not harder. People will no longer be able find high-paying jobs nor be qualified for these jobs with a minimal education. Because most of the education is rote memorization the students are unprepared for the real world. Students in high school can not balance a check book or fill out a simple DMV form, but these are skills they will need for the rest of their life. Why have classes in pottery and home economics when you need to know PowerPoint, Word, and Excel if you want your resume to even be looked at by a prospective employer. Why not have a child really prepared to join today's real workforce after they accept their diploma? Isn't that the point of this system? A system which is neither educating students, nor preparing them for real life. In short we are turning out an expensive product that is unprepared, ill suited and unwanted in the global job marketplace. This absolutely has to change.

Obviously the concept of lumping everyone into grades is not working well, since some children will learn faster and be bored and unchallenged and some learn slower and will never catch up. The way tests are used in useless, there is no follow up or mechanism for filling in what was missed. We do not need to reinvent the wheel here, don't continue to throw more money at what is not working, what is working in Europe? Bring it here. What is working at college level here? Study it and copy it. Why don't private schools have these problems? Being rich does not make you smart. Kevin P. Chavous is a noted author and national school reform leader. As a former member of the Council of the District of Columbia and Chair of the Council's Committee on Education, Libraries and Recreation, Mr. Chavous was at the forefront of promoting change within the District public school system and was able to get educational results in his schools which were considered impossible by the district. He is a strong advocate for vouchers. Instead of copying what Kevin Chavous is doing and trying to replicate it and get better results everywhere the school system ignores him.

Unlike jobs in the private sector where you are given a yearly evaluation and ranked and rated against your peers for review, based upon your individual performance you are given a raise. It may surprise you to know that this scenario does not exist for school teachers. Teachers are not ranked or rated against their peers. Teachers do not get a raise based upon their individual effort or performance. Teachers receive a merit increase based upon what their union has negotiated for that period. All teachers receive the same increase based on length of service. So you see there is no financial incentive to be the best teacher in the school, or the best teacher in the district or the best teacher in the country for that matter, because you will get the same increase as the worst teacher in the district. So why would a teacher bend over backwards for students, provide supplementary learning materials, work extra hours and weekends when at the end of the year he will get the same exact raise as the teacher who came in late, left early and generally could not give a rats ass what his classes did. Other than personal pride there is no reason, but we do not pay people or reward them for personal pride. This not meant to stereotype all teachers because certainly there are many great teachers out there who do not do all that they do for money, but why put in and maintain a system like this? A Socialist reward system for a Socialist school system one that rewards mediocrity and achieves Socialist results.

The primary issue of why the schools systems are failing and do such a disservice to everyone is that the tax money for education is tied to the zip code and not tied to the child. Why can't you send your child to the best school instead of one that is failing? Teachers do not like the idea of vouchers because it threatens them; it will force them to do their jobs something they are largely insulated from doing through the benefits of their union with tenure and seniority. If your school is the worst school in the nation and I wanted to send my child somewhere else, I can't. Why can't I, it is my tax money? So your worst school will never be fixed, it never has to be fixed, because it will continue to get money based on the zip code, it can stay broken forever. Competition is the American way and this archaic

Socialist institution is completed insulated from it and look at the results. This zip code concept represents a major portion (60%) of the education systems problems. While no teacher wants to be responsible for a child that does not want to learn, that being said these children are the exception not the rule. On the other hand no parent wants a teacher that doesn't give a shit, is not paid to give a shit, in a school system that does not give a shit and the reason they can choose to not give a shit is because you have no choice of where you can send your child (paid for by your tax money) if this is your zip code then this is your school. They do not have to give a shit because if you do not like it that is too bad, there is no competition, no choices, no alternatives and short of expensive private school there is nothing you can do about it and it's your money. Tying the money to the zip code has got us to where we are today with our current education system obviously we are in dire need of a new method that promotes competition and values learning. Trying something different could not possibly yield any worse results that the current 15 year trend of the education system.

But don't just take my word for it, let's see what a top Fortune 50 CEO thinks of the education system. Here is a recent piece from the Washington Times. Steve Jobs, the co-founder and CEO of Apple, just lost any friends he had in the executive offices of the nation's teacher unions. Speaking recently at an education reform conference in Austin, Mr. Jobs blamed the unionization of America's public schools for much of what's wrong with today's public education system.
"What kind of person could you get to run a small business," he asked, comparing school principals to CEOs, "if you told them that when they came in they couldn't get rid of people that they thought weren't any good?"

Unfortunately for America's schoolchildren, Mr. Jobs' criticisms are just scraping the surface.

Across America, there are more than 3 million public-school teachers. Organized through the National Education Association and the American Federation of Teachers -- the nation's two largest labor unions -- they wield enormous political influence and aren't afraid to use it. Much of this power comes through the dues that union leaders deduct from teachers' paychecks, supposedly to improve the working conditions of the teachers they represent. In California, for example, the state teachers' association represents 340,000 workers and collects more than $150 million each year in mandatory dues.

But in reality, the unions often promote an agenda that doesn't reflect the interests of their members. Performance-based pay for teachers is a prime example of how the unions work directly against their members' own best interests. In inner-city schools, the best teachers often leave after just a year or two for better salaries, nicer neighborhoods and less stressful work. Merit pay, however, makes it possible for these schools to retain effective teachers by paying them more. But the unions usually fight tooth and nail against such measures.

By standing against proven reform, the union agenda also harms the nation's schoolchildren.

Using member dues, unions regularly lobby against efforts to allow students trapped in underperforming schools to transfer to better schools by using vouchers. Never mind the fact that study after study has demonstrated that voucher systems boost student achievement in both public and private schools, regardless of socioeconomic background.

By David White March 12, 2007 http://www.washingtontimes.com/

SOURCE: U.S. Department of Education, National Center for Education Statistics (2006). *Digest of Education Statistics, 2005* (NCES 2006–030).

Average reading scale score, by age, sex, and race/ethnicity: Selected years, 1971 to 2004								
Sex and race/ethnicity	**1971**	**1975**	**1980**	**1984**	**1990**	**1994**	**1999**	**2004**
9-year-olds[1]								
Total	208	210	215	211	209	211	212	219
Male	201	204	210	207	204	207	209	216
Female	214	216	220	214	215	215	215	221
Race/ethnicity								
White, non-Hispanic	214	217	221	218	217	218	221	226
Black, non-Hispanic	170	181	189	186	182	185	186	200
Hispanic	(1)	183	190	187	189	186	193	205
13-year-olds								
Total	255	256	258	257	257	258	259	259
Male	250	250	254	253	251	251	254	254
Female	261	262	263	262	263	266	265	264
Race/ethnicity								
White, non-Hispanic	261	262	264	263	262	265	267	266

Black, non-Hispanic	222	226	233	236	241	234	238	244
Hispanic	(1)	232	237	240	238	235	244	242
17-year-olds								
Total	285	286	285	289	290	288	288	285
Male	279	280	282	284	284	282	281	278
Female	291	291	289	294	296	295	295	292
Race/ethnicity								
White, non-Hispanic	291	293	293	295	297	296	295	293
Black, non-Hispanic	239	241	243	264	267	266	264	264
Hispanic	(1)	252	261	268	275	263	271	264

SHOW ME THE IMPROVEMENT ? 35 Years, Trillions of dollars

NOTE: The NAEP scores have been evaluated at certain performance levels. Scale ranges from 0 to 500. Students at reading score level 150 are able to follow brief written directions and carry out simple, discrete reading tasks. **SOURCE:** U.S. Department of Education, National Center for Education Statistics (2006). *Digest of Education Statistics, 2005* (NCES 2006–030), **Table 108**.

Compared to middle and high school students, younger students are making the most progress in science. In 2005, a representative sample of more than 300,000 students in grades 4, 8, and 12 was assessed in science. This report presents national results for all three grades, and state results for grades 4 and 8. The 2005 results are compared to those from 1996 and 2000. Sample questions are presented to illustrate the types of skills and knowledge that were assessed at each grade.

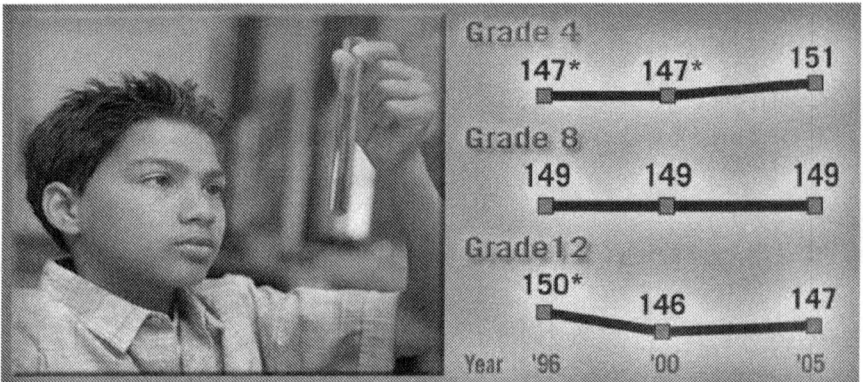

* Significantly different from 2005.
SOURCE: U.S. Department of Education, Institute of Education Sciences, National Center for Education Statistics, National Assessment of Educational Progress (NAEP), 1996, 2000, and 2005 Science Assessments.

Again 25 pages of rhetoric and drivel for lackluster results, we spend more money on education every year, devise new curriculums, new teaching methods, and improve technology in every school for NO results.

Students at reading score level 200 are able to understand, combine ideas, and make inferences based on short uncomplicated passages about specific or sequentially related information. Students at reading score level 250 are able to search for specific information, interrelate ideas, and make generalizations about literature, science, and social studies materials. Students at reading score level 300 are able to find, understand, summarize, and explain relatively complicated literary and informational material. Includes public and private schools. Excludes persons not enrolled in school and those who were unable to be tested due to limited proficiency in English or due to a disability. Some data have been revised from previously published figures. Standard errors appear in parentheses.

The SAT (formerly known as the Scholastic Assessment Test and the Scholastic Aptitude Test) is not designed as an indicator of student achievement, but rather as an aid for predicting how well students will do in college. Between 1995–96 and 2005–06, mathematics SAT scores increased by 10 points, 2007-017),

SAT score averages of college-bound seniors, by race/ethnicity: Selected years, 1990-91 through 2005-06							
Race/ethnicity	1990-91	1996-97	2000-01	2001-02	2002-03	2003-04	2004-05	2005-06
SAT-Critical reading								
All students	499	505	506	504	507	508	508	503
White	518	526	529	527	529	528	532	527
Black	427	434	433	430	431	430	433	434
Hispanic or Latino	458	466	460	458	457	461	463	458

Mexican American	454	451	451	446	448	451	453	454
Puerto Rican	436	454	457	455	456	457	460	459
Asian	485	496	501	501	508	507	511	510
American Indian	470	475	481	479	480	483	489	487
Other	486	512	503	502	501	494	495	494

SAT-Mathematics

All students	500	511	514	516	519	518	520	518
White	513	526	531	533	534	531	536	536
Black	419	423	426	427	426	427	431	429
Hispanic or Latino	462	468	465	464	464	465	469	463
Mexican American	459	458	458	457	457	458	463	465
Puerto Rican	439	447	451	451	453	452	457	456
Asian	548	560	566	569	575	577	580	578
American Indian	468	475	479	483	482	488	493	494
Other	492	514	512	514	513	508	513	513

Written proof of 15 years with a severe lack of progress.

THE FUTURE

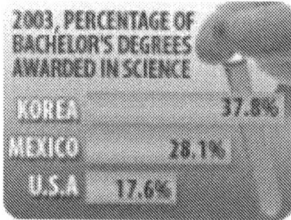

2003, Percentage of bachelor's degrees awarded in science, by country:

Korea - 37.8%

Mexico - 28.1%

U.S.A. - 17.6%   The numbers for Engineering look worse

The reporting of engineering graduation data has fueled fears that America is losing its technological edge. Media reports have stated that in 2004 the United States produced 70,000 engineering graduates while China graduated 600,000 and India 350,000.
http://www3.nsta.org/main/news/stories/nsta_story.php?news_story_ID =52016 NSTA while these totals have been under scrutiny even if the foreign numbers are halved it still points in one direction.

Nearly 50 million students are heading off to approximately 97,000 public elementary and secondary schools for the fall term, and before the school year is out, an estimated $489 billion will be spent related to their education. (For an Average of $9,970 per pupil)

How Students performed on National Reading and Math Tests

The National Assessment of Educational Progress (NAEP) also known as "the Nation's Report Card," is the only nationally representative and continuing assessment of what American students know and can do it reading and math. NAEP results are based on a sample of the states students.

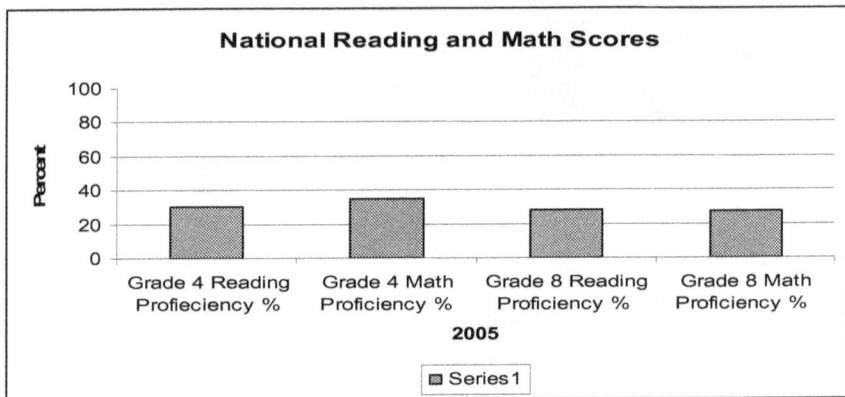

National Reading and Math Scores

	Grade 4 Reading Profiency %	Grade 4 Math Proficiency %	Grade 8 Reading Proficiency %	Grade 8 Math Proficiency %
2005				

Series1

Finding relevant information is not easy and results are biased

Spending Summary

Total allocation of resources and spending per child

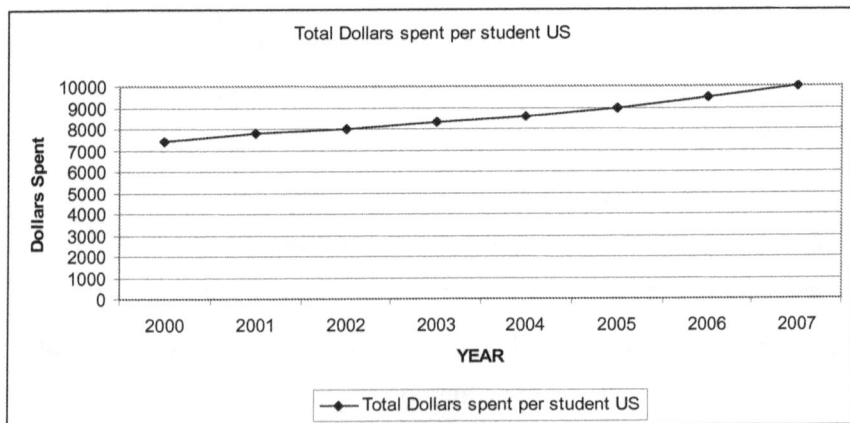

Total Dollars spent per student US

— Total Dollars spent per student US

More Money no Results, the mystery of "more money less results" continues.

DESTROYING AMERICA

Chapter 9 - The IRS - Tax Time for your 120,000 friends at the IR_asS
9,000 pages of loop holes, gray areas and lies

The freedoms won by Americans in 1776 were lost in the revolution of 1913. Richard E. Byrd, speaker of the Virginia House of Delegates, predicted, "a hand from Washington will be stretched out and placed upon every man's business. . . . Heavy fines imposed by distant and unfamiliar tribunals will constantly menace the taxpayer. An army of Federal officials, spies and detectives will descend upon the state. . . ." Pandora had opened the box. And he was right. Our entire country came about upon the idea that taxation without representation was wrong., oh how far the apple has fallen.

Most people can not remember a time when there were no taxes, because nowadays everything in our country is taxed. But back before 1913 there was no income tax, and the government managed to get by for 137 years without taxing the people. There were taxes back then but not on the income of the people. Some really dirty politicians put together an amendment sponsored by the banks to tax ordinary citizens. As always the tax started really small and unobtrusive and it only applied to the super rich! Once a tax law is passed from then on only one thing happens the rate goes up, and who is applies to gets broader. This how the US income tax came to into existence.

When the first income tax was sent out to the people, the Congress chortled confidently that "all good citizen will willingly and cheerfully support and sustain this, the fairest and cheapest of all taxes." That was the cute little

monkey part.   In 1913 the Secretary of State Philanderer Knox (perfect
name) was a lame duck politician on his way out of office in his last week in
office when the 16th Amendment was mysteriously ratified, and he wound
up in the employ of the bankers who drafted it. From How the Cute Little
Monkey Grew into a Gorilla (1994 data)

After all, the first tax ranged from merely 1% on the first $20,000 of taxable
income and was only 7% on incomes above $500,000. Who could
complain? The $20,000 is the equivalent of someone who earns $250,000
today and the $500,000 is equivalent to some who earns over $6 million
dollars today.   So basically it was a luxury tax on the uber-rich! So you did
not know you were uber-rich?!

At first, scarcely anyone paid income tax. Little did they know that before
the tinkering was done in Washington, this system would be described by
many Americans as the most unfair and expensive tax in the history of the
nation. Within a few years, it had become the principal source of income for
the federal government. In the beginning, hardly anyone had to file a tax
return because the tax did not apply to the vast majority of America's work-
a-day citizens.

For example, in 1939, 26 years after the Sixteenth Amendment was adopted,
only 5% of the population, counting both taxpayers and their dependents,
was required to file returns. Today, more than 85% of the population is
under the income tax. 26 years after it was passed it applied to LESS than
5% of the US population, by and large it was hidden and applied to no one.
All the while they continued to increase the tax rate and lower the income
requirements, those smart little government bastards. As late as 1940, fewer

than fifteen million tax returns were filed. Just ten years later in 1950, the number would be fifty-three million. Adjusting for inflation, in the 81 years between the enactments of the income tax amendment in 1913 to 1994, government spending increased 13,592%.

The Supreme Court has gone back and forth that the 16th amendment conferred no new powers of taxation on the government. The Supreme Court in the 1916 decision of Stanton vs. Baltic Mining stated that "by the previous ruling (Brushaber vs. Union Pacific) it was settled that the provisions of the Sixteenth Amendment conferred no new power of taxation but simply prohibited 'power of income taxation' from being taken out of the category of indirect taxation to which it inherently belonged" (qtd. in Robbins). The Brushaber decision reasserted that government was not granted infinite taxing authority and that an income tax is indirect and thus inapplicable to individuals who do not engage in the specified taxable activities.

So let me get out my crayons and see if I understand this, the Income Tax amendment that was never legally ratified (see below) so technically, to this day, it should not be a law and it is under challenge. But lets say it did pass, the Income Tax was meant to be 1% of the income of those who earned $250,000 per year and even 26 years after it was passed only applied to 5% of the population. Wow so how did we get so lucky?

Also put this in perspective at the time the 16th Amendment was "almost" ratified in 1913 there were: NO STATE TAXES, NO SALES TAXES, NO FICA, NO SOCIAL SECURITY, No Medicare and no Real estate taxes, or that would have been considered part of the burden. Aren't we lucky! Look at the monster we have created. Now half of our workday's earnings go to pay our taxes. Tax "Freedom Day" is based on the number of days Americans work to pay taxes to the number of days they work to support themselves. Tax Freedom Day in 2007 was April 30, 2 days later than 2006, as it continues to move further and further into the year.

"Americans will work longer to pay for government (120 days) than they will for food, clothing and housing combined (105 days)," said Hodge. "Since 1986 taxes have cost more than these basic necessities. In fact, Americans will work longer to afford federal taxes alone (79 days) than they will to afford housing (62 days)."

In 2007 Americans will work another 41 days to afford their state and local taxes. That makes taxation a bigger financial burden than housing and household operation (62 days), health and medical care (52 days), food (30 days), transportation (30 days), recreation (22 days), or clothing and accessories (13 days).

The IRS a growing beast

IRS Facts 120,000 Employees $11.5 Billion dollar budget 90% is labor costs IRS Prints and mails 280 instructional forms for the various IRS documents the tax code is 9,000 pages long with 90 years of special interests on every page.

Yet another US growth industry. A US House study puts the cost of compliance at $125 Billion annually 2004- Saxton-109-11-7-05. Roughly 15% of all revenue collected. Of this $300 Billion dollar gap, between collection and amount owed (a large portion of the "gap" are penalties) that is a primary focus of the 120,000 IRS employees; penalties are due by and large to under payment because of complexity and interpretation of the tax code. go to 10 different accountants get 10 different returns. In 2006 they collected $49 Billion dollars or 16% of the "gap" amount owed (but only $34 B in 2002) Assuming a 75% labor cost ratio on un-collected amounts, the direct related costs are over $9 Billion dollars (+compliance costs) to collect $49 Billion, or 20%-40% inefficiency and waste. It basically costs us almost .35c to collect .20c. or $300 Billion dollars owed, we spend $9 B to collect $40 B of it. Ah, government math.

We do not need 120,000 IRS employees, and penalties, and strange interpretations that need to be reviewed, we need a flat tax, pay X% or your earnings. No gray area no need for 120,000 employees. A FLAT TAX ELIMINATES 95% of these issues. Links and footnotes are in the reference section.

Every year we see Geraldo or a local group of investigative reporters take a "standard family of four" tax return to several different CPAs firms. And every year they get a different return back and different amounts of tax owed or refund due from each CPA firm. If they went to 50 different places they would get 50 different tax returns back based on the same information. Nothing that is this inaccurate and vague with this amount of gray areas should be considered a law. When a cop pulls you over for speeding he definitively tells you how fast you were going. Moreover one of the primary sources of IRS income are the penalties, penalties with rates and surcharges you could not get away with in the private sector. How can you penalize someone on the amount of tax they pay when you can not get 3 tax professionals to agree on the same number on what you should be paying? No one would pass a law that read you could be arrested if you are out after dark its too vague. But it's OK to say here read through these 9000 pages of tax code and figure out what you owe.

Simplify the Code

The US Tax code 9,000 pages, replete with loopholes galore for those who pay for them, it has been amended 14,000 times since Reagan left office. Let us look at reality unless you paid for a loophole none of these 9,000 pages really apply to you. This not a tax code "by the people, for the people" this is a tax code by the special interests on the people. "Unfortunately, however, most of us are hardly aware of the tremendous burden that tax complexity imposes a burden that largely manifests itself in higher consumer prices. On average, between 20 percent and 25 percent of the price of consumer goods is the price of our tax code, tax compliance and tax avoidance. For example, one dollar's worth of gasoline includes 48 cents in taxes and a $1.14 loaf of bread includes 35 cents in taxes. Studies have shown that, if we simplified our system through fundamental tax reform, we would eliminate this component in the price system and thereby increase purchasing power by more than 20 percent." Tax Reform Experts

Steve Forbes : "My flat tax plan has one simple rate, on the federal level: 17% on personal income and 17% on corporate profits. There would be generous exemptions for individuals: $13,200 for each adult; $4,000 for each child or dependent, and a refundable tax credit of $1,000 per child 16 or younger. A family of four would pay no federal income tax on its first $46,165 of income. Exemptions for a family of six--mom, dad, four kids-- would be $65,930. No anti-risk-taking capital gains levy; the capital gains tax would go to zero.

The abusive Alternative Minimum (really maximum) Tax would be

abolished. No more death tax: You'd leave the world unmolested by the IRS.
No taxation without respiration!" There are other simple tax plans with
similar ideas if you do not trust Forbes
http://www.scrapthecode.com/facts.htm   Both are members of Congress 2
different ideas both better than current pile of shit.

More comments from Forbes:
Other countries are getting the message, even if we have yet to. Hong Kong
has successfully had a variation of the flat tax for 60 years. Lithuania, Latvia
and Estonia enacted flat taxes in the 1990s that have been hugely successful.
Russia put in a flat tax four years ago, and revenues have more than doubled
in real terms. Ukraine, Slovakia, Romania, Georgia and Serbia have also
successfully enacted flat taxes. How ironic that one time Communist nations
have been reaping the benefits of a flat tax before that bastion of free
enterprise, the U.S.
President Bush should understand that trying to tinker with the tax beast
won't work. In 1986, Ronald Reagan simplified the tax code somewhat: A
number of tax shelters were eliminated and the numbers of tax brackets
were cut to two: 28% and 15%. But the code remained intact. No sooner
was the ink of Reagan's signature dry than Washington politicians slid back
into their bad, old habits. Since his day,(Reagan) the federal income tax
code has been amended 14,000 times.
The tax system today is 60% larger than it was after the Reagan reforms.
The flat tax's very simplicity makes such backsliding difficult: Any change
would trigger a national debate. For insurance, the Forbes Flat Tax also
contains a supermajority provision--taxes can't be raised unless approved by
a 60% vote in both the House and Senate. Few tax boosts in recent decades
have surmounted such a barrier. The usual objections to the flat tax don't

hold up. The flat tax will help housing--personal incomes would go up and interest rates would go down--and boost charitable giving. Experience demonstrates that when people earn more they give more, and will spend more.

What a former IRS Commissioner thinks of the income tax.
A Former IRS Commissioner's Statement (You will not see this on the IRS homepage)

T. Coleman Andrews served as commissioner of IRS for 3 years during the early 1950s. Following his resignation, he made the following statement:
"Congress [in implementing the Sixteenth Amendment] went beyond merely enacting an income tax law and repealed Article IV of the Bill of Rights, by empowering the tax collector to do the very things from which that article says we were to be secure. It opened up our homes, our papers and our effects to the prying eyes of government agents and set the stage for searches of our books and vaults and for inquiries into our private affairs whenever the tax men might decide, even though there might not be any justification beyond mere cynical suspicion."
"The income tax is bad because it has robbed you and me of the guarantee of privacy and the respect for our property that were given to us in Article IV of the Bill of Rights. This invasion is absolute and complete as far as the amount of tax that can be assessed is concerned. Please remember that under the Sixteenth Amendment, Congress can take 100% of our income anytime it wants to. As a matter of fact, right now it is imposing a tax as high as 91%. This is downright confiscation and cannot be defended on any other grounds."
"The income tax is bad because it was conceived in class hatred, is an

instrument of vengeance and plays right into the hands of the communists. It employs the vicious communist principle of taking from each according to his accumulation of the fruits of his labor and giving to others according to their needs, regardless of whether those needs are the result of indolence or lack of pride, self-respect, personal dignity or other attributes of men."

"The income tax is fulfilling the Marxist prophecy that the surest way to destroy a capitalist society is by steeply graduated taxes on income and heavy levies upon the estates of people when they die."

[As matters now stand, if our children make the most of their capabilities and training, they will have to give most of it to the tax collector and so become slaves of the government. People cannot pull themselves up by the bootstraps anymore because the tax collector gets the boots and the straps as well.]

"The income tax is bad because it is oppressive to all and discriminates particularly against those people who prove themselves most adept at keeping the wheels of business turning and creating maximum employment and a high standard of living for their fellow men."

"I believe that a better way to raise revenue not only can be found but must be found because I am convinced that the present system is leading us right back to the very tyranny from which those, who established this land of freedom, risked their lives, their fortunes and their sacred honor to forever free themselves..."

Income Tax was kind of approved

CAVEAT this still falls under urban legend but is worth reading.

Of Interest, Income Tax provision technically was never approved

Article V of the U.S. Constitution specifies the ratification process, and requires 3/4 of the States to ratify any amendment proposed by Congress. There were 48 States in the American Union in 1913, meaning that affirmative action of 36 states was required for ratification. In February, 1913, Secretary of State Philander Knox issued a proclamation claiming that 38 states had ratified the amendment. In 1984, William J. Benson began a research project, never before performed, to investigate the process of ratification of the 16th Amendment. After traveling to the capitols of the New England states, and reviewing the journals of the state legislative bodies, he saw that many states had not ratified the Amendment. Continuing his research at the National Archives in Washington, DC, Bill Benson discovered his Golden Key. This damning piece of evidence is a 16 page memorandum from the Solicitor of the Department of State, whose duty is the provision of legal opinions for the use of the Secretary of State. In this memorandum sent to the Secretary of State, the Solicitor of the Department of State lists the many errors he found in the ratification process!

The 4 states listed

The Kentucky Senate voted upon the resolution, but rejected it by a vote of 9 in favor and 22 opposed.
The Oklahoma Senate amended the language of the 16th Amendment to have a precisely opposite meaning.
The California legislative assembly never recorded any vote upon any proposal to adopt the amendment proposed by Congress.

The State of Minnesota sent nothing to the Secretary of State in Washington. When his year long project was finished at the end of 1984, Bill had visited every state capitol and knew that not a single state had actually and legally ratified the proposal to amend the Constitution. 33 states engaged in the unauthorized activity of amending the language of the amendment proposed by congress, a power the states do not possess. Since 36 states were needed for ratification, the failure of 13 to ratify would be fatal to the amendment, and this occurs within the major (first three) defects tabulated in Defects in Ratification of the 16th Amendment. Even if we were to ignore defects of spelling, capitalization, and punctuation, we would still have only 2 states which successfully ratified. He has been tied up in court since 1984 Hmmmmm, I wonder why?

Twelve other states violated provisions in their State Constitutions, bringing the number down to 21. Philander Knox, a lame duck politician the Secretary of State, 1909-1913, for the Taft Administration, proclaimed the 16th amendment to be ratified just a few days before he left office in 1913 to make way for the Wilson administration, even though he knew it had not been legally ratified. Philander Knox had for many years been the primary attorney for the richest men in America, including Carnegie, Rockefeller, Morgan, the Vanderbilts, the Mellons, and others. He had created for them the largest cartel in the world, then was appointed, at their request, as the Attorney General in the McKinley/Roosevelt administrations, where he refused to enforce the Sherman anti-trust laws against the cartel he had just created.

IRS to be less kinder and gentler
WASHINGTON - "Think of the uses of $300 billion, the annual gap between what taxpayers owe and what they pay. It would more than cover the federal deficit for a year or the extra money President Bush wants in 2007 and 2008 for Iraq and Afghanistan. It would pay for the $125 billion that Congress has agreed to spend on Hurricane Katrina relief, with enough left for three years worth of federal education programs."

Yes, Yes think of the uses of $300 Billion dollars, another war in a random country, another Skylab or Hubble telescope which we will not maintain and will let fall out of the sky, a couple bridges to nowhere, we could give more American weapons to Iraq or Iran or a random country to use against us, another Yucca mountain, Railroad to nowhere, lots of tanks and missiles, $400 hammers, a few months of interest on the National Debt from all those years of responsible spending! This is why news organizations should not do puff pastry pieces, lets not examine how messed up the machine is lets get those dirty tax cheaters! What does the US government need another $300 Billion dollars for? Show us what you did with the last $300 Billion dollars.

How many IRS Employees does it take to screw in a light bulb?
"Unlike other federal agencies, the IRS has a nearly $2 billion collection budget with thousands of collection employees," the report said. "In contrast, PCAs ... are using 75 employees to collect on these accounts, and the IRS is using 65 employees to monitor them. The IRS with its vast resources can do what 75 PCA employees can do." They are using 65 employees to monitor 75 people. You cant make this stuff up.

Government to Impose Excise TAX to pay for WAR
1898 , When I tell you once a tax gets approved it never goes away.
3% Federal Excise Tax on your phone bill was imposed to pay for the Spanish American WAR

The WAR HAS BEEN OVER FOR 107 YEARS

NEW YORK — Some say it's absurd. According to seven federal courts, it's also illegal. But one thing is for sure: America's excise tax on phone service has soaked consumers for more than a century. Rep. Gary Miller, R-Calif., recently introduced legislation in the House — supported by 98 co-sponsors — aimed at repealing the tax, which was imposed in 1898 to help pay for the Spanish-American War. The war was over in six months, but the tax stayed. The general excise tax has so far cost consumers about $300 billion, says the Congressional Research Service. The entire Spanish-American War cost only about $6 billion, adjusted for inflation. $300 Billion dollars!

Tax Freedom Day, 1980-2007 (click for larger image)

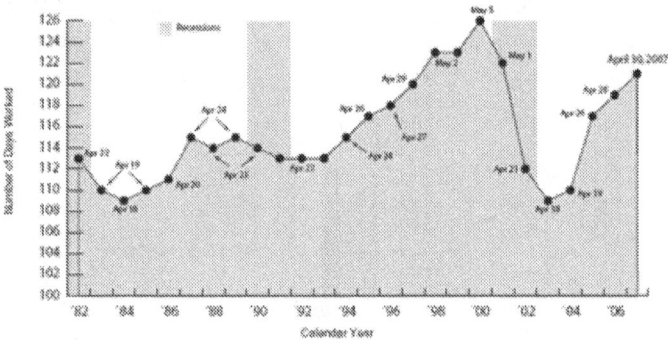

http://www.taxfoundation.org/taxfreedomday/

Figure 4
Average Number of Days Worked to Pay Taxes by Type of Tax and Level of Government
Calendar Year 2007

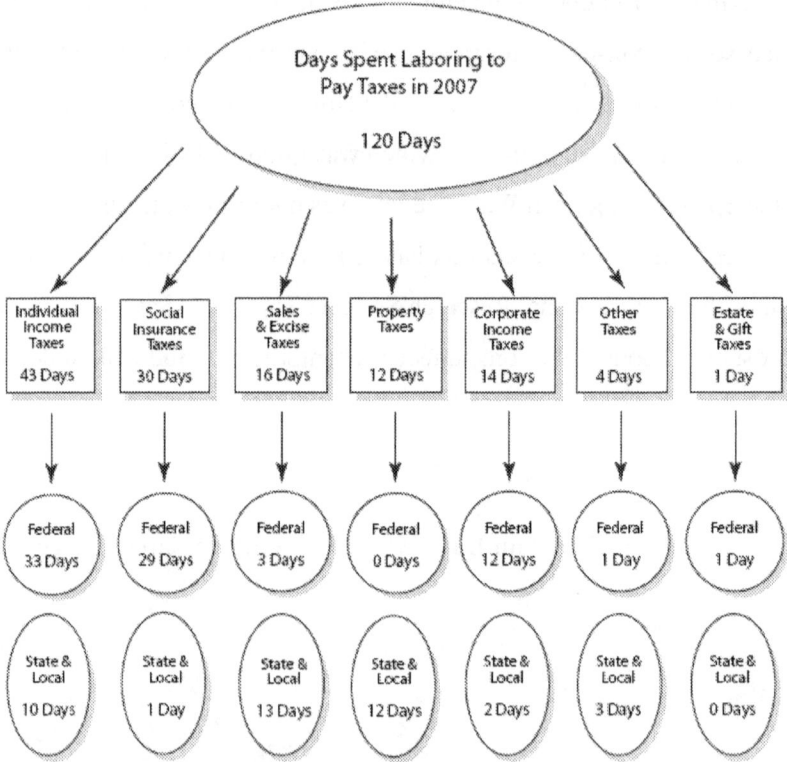

```
            Days Spent Laboring to
             Pay Taxes in 2007

                  120 Days
```

Individual Income Taxes	Social Insurance Taxes	Sales & Excise Taxes	Property Taxes	Corporate Income Taxes	Other Taxes	Estate & Gift Taxes
43 Days	30 Days	16 Days	12 Days	14 Days	4 Days	1 Day
Federal 33 Days	Federal 29 Days	Federal 3 Days	Federal 0 Days	Federal 12 Days	Federal 1 Day	Federal 1 Day
State & Local 10 Days	State & Local 1 Day	State & Local 13 Days	State & Local 12 Days	State & Local 2 Days	State & Local 3 Days	State & Local 0 Days

2007 (click to enlarge)

Figure 1
How Long America Works to Pay Taxes in Days Compared to
Other Major Spending Categories
Calendar Year 2007

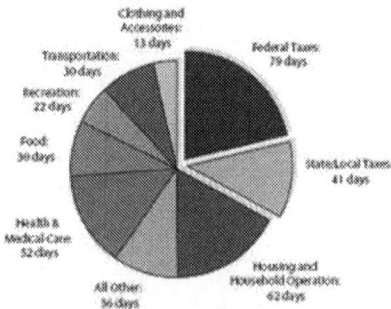

Clothing and Accessories: 13 days
Transportation: 30 days
Recreation: 22 days
Food: 30 days
Health & Medical Care: 52 days
All Other: 36 days
Federal Taxes: 79 days
State/Local Taxes: 41 days
Housing and Household Operation: 62 days

Table 1: Tax Freedom Day and Tax Burden, Selected Years 1900 - 2007		
Year	Tax Freedom Day	Taxes as a Percentage of Income
1900	22-Jan	5.90%
1910	19-Jan	5.02%
1920	13-Feb	11.96%
1930	12-Feb	11.61%
1940	7-Mar	17.98%
1950	01-Apr	24.87%
1960	12-Apr	27.88%
1970	20-Apr	29.90%
1980	22-Apr	30.68%
1990	23-Apr	30.80%
2000	5-May	33.98%
2001	1-May	33.01%
2002	21-Apr	30.27%
2003	18-Apr	29.51%
2004	19-Apr	29.69%
2005	26-Apr	31.53%
2006	28-Apr	32.29%
2007	30-Apr	32.69%

Source: Office of Management and Budget; Internal Revenue Service; Congressional Research Service; National Bureau of Economic Research;

There are many better ideas out there that are much, much better than anything you will see from the IRS, here are just 2 examples.

http://www.scrapthecode.com/facts.htm

Individual Tax Freedom Act

The Individual Tax Freedom Act is sponsored by Congressman Billy Tauzin (R) of Louisiana's 3rd congressional district.

- The sales tax would be 15%
- Abolishes the Internal Revenue Service
- Eliminates federal income tax withholding; you keep more of your paycheck (an instant pay raise)
- Eliminates estate, inheritance and gift taxes, and eliminates most excise taxes; your children can receive *all* of your estate
- Eliminates hidden taxes in the prices for goods (pre-tax prices fall)
- Poor families would be protected with rebates deducted from FICA taxes
- Non-working poor collecting a federal subsidy would receive an increase in their subsidy to offset the tax
- Tax on housing is amortized over 30 years; you would receive a credit when selling your house
- Collects tax revenues now lost to the underground "cash economy"
- Collection would be done by the states (45 states already administer a sales tax)
- Each state would receive 1% of the taxes collected to offset collection costs

- Businesses would receive .5% of the taxes collected to offset their collection costs
- Social Security Administration would collect Social Security payments and Medicare tax

The FairTax

The FairTax bill is sponsored by Congressman John Linder (R) of Georgia's 7th congressional district and co-sponsored by Congressman Collin Peterson (D) of Minnesota's 7th congressional district.

- Imposes a 23% (tax-inclusive) sales tax on the purchase of new goods and services in the U.S.
- Lets workers keep their **entire paycheck** and retirees keep their entire pension.
- Abolishes the IRS and ends all audits of individual taxpayers.
- Replaces the federal income tax. Frees individuals from ever filing a tax return again.
- Replaces all payroll taxes including Social Security and Medicare taxes. Current Social Security and Medicare benefits would not change.
- Replaces corporate and self-employment taxes.
- Eliminates all hidden federal taxes.
- Provides a universal rebate equal to the sales taxes paid on essential goods and services to ensure that no American pays taxes on necessities.
- Replaces all estate, gift, and capital gains taxes.
- Dramatically lowers tax rates for low- and middle-income Americans.

- Closes all tax loopholes.
- Brings accountability to tax policy.
- Lets American-made products compete fairly.

DESTROYING AMERICA

Chapter 10 - The Tent Stakes of Stupidity

What follows here are the "major" issues that divide the parties, the Liberal Democrats from the Conservative Republicans. Bear in mind that labels, stereotyping and name calling all serves to keep stupidity firmly entrenched and rational thinking very far away. In no particular order: Capital Punishment, Abortion, Gun Control, Pledge of Allegiance (the word "God" being included), teaching evolution in schools (Darwin) etc, with Gay Marriage and Medically Assisted suicide poking their head in from time to time and as of late "Intelligent Design". Everyone has their hot button on this list, their little pet peeve argument but everything in this category just serves as a distraction, nothing more. It's the freak show outside of the big tent because as I will detail none of these issues will solve any of the real problems in America. You are going to the big show and you wind up looking at the tent stakes. These arguments are the moral equivalent of a car accident victim coming into the Emergency room on a stretcher with serious injuries and you as the surgeon give the patient a manicure as he dies. Lets treat the major head wound and stop the bleeding we have been quibbling over the useless noise for 200 years.

Capital Punishment, this is a belief that bad people, who commit double, triple homicide and heinous murders should be given the death penalty and executed by the state. The counter argument is that lethal injection or electrocutions are "cruel and unusual" punishment, which is banned by the

8th Amendment in the Bill of Rights in 1787. I can tell you that the preferred method of execution in the time of our forefathers: Adams, Jefferson, Franklin and such was hanging the criminal. Also criminals were drawn and quartered. This where each limb being is tied to four different horses and somebody yelling Giddy Up!! Since that was not considered cruel and unusual punishment then I surely do not think the equivalent of taking a sleeping pill is. In reality the average death row inmate sits on death row 25 years waiting for execution filing appeal after appeal running up the cost of death row inmates, they cost is up to 70% higher per year for death row inmates. California published a number that each execution of a death row inmate including appeals cost the taxpayers $250 million dollars in the March 6, 2005 Los Angeles Times. So I do not know if eliminating the Death penalty really has any real impact since no one seems to actually die, and those that do are not exactly honor student types. I know that two wrongs don't make a right, and the family gets closure, nothing will bring back the victim, etc, etc, so as you can see this subject goes nowhere fast. There are currently 3350 people on death row in the United States. 53 people were executed in 2006 and 1100 people total since 1976 when the states could opt for having a death penalty. 12 states do not have a death penalty. So unless you plan on being a triple murderer this probably is not going to affect you. But the political parties will spend a whole lot of time on this and the Republicans look tough on crime, when actually almost no one is being executed and certainly not swiftly, average time on death row is 20+ years and it also seems that almost 2/3 of executions are race related. Killing this human garbage solves almost nothing and leaving them in prison to rot solves almost nothing, but economically speaking why flush $250 Million dollars down a rat hole?

Here is a great example of one of the pillars of the community now 25 years on death row.

Michael Morales was condemned in 1983 for killing 17-year-old Terri Winchell, who was attacked with a hammer, stabbed and left to die half-naked in a vineyard. Did we mention the part about running her over with his car (twice) on the way out just for good measure. Morales the stable citizen that he was, had plotted the killing with a gay cousin who was jealous of Winchell's relationship with another man. The cousin was sentenced to life in prison without parole.

'Totally disillusioned' The victim's mother, Barbara Christian, was outraged by the repeated delays. "I'm totally disillusioned with the justice system. We've been waiting 25 years with the expectancy that he is gonna pay for his crimes," she said. "It feels like we just got punched in the stomach." So Morales has a new attorney who is questioning the "cruel and unusual" aspects of a lethal injection. Hanging and being drawn and quartered was pretty standard for the guys that wrote the constitution, so I don't know how an injection that puts you to sleep would be more painful than snapping your head off with a rope but leave it up to a trial lawyer to try to prove it $1,000 per minute of the systems time.

Here is a person that would not have earned $1 million dollars over his lifetime so even at a 30% tax bracket he would paid $300,000 into the system (hypothetically) over the last 25 years between trials, appeals, court time, lawyers, and housing and medical care he has cost the citizen probably close to $100 million dollars in total costs including man hours. And while I am really glad the attorneys have worried about his civil rights and if lethal injection is too cruel a form punishment, but of those of us not living in the ethical elitist Ivory tower, I would like to know the answer to one thing for my portion of the $100M in tax money spent on him.

Did anyone ask him if the girl he killed consider being hit in the back of the head 23 times with a claw hammer? Cruel and unusual ?

If not, Do you think raping, stabbing and running her over with your car was cruel and unusual?
Leaving this un-human thing alive for 25 years is cruel and unusual.

Death Row Executions per Year

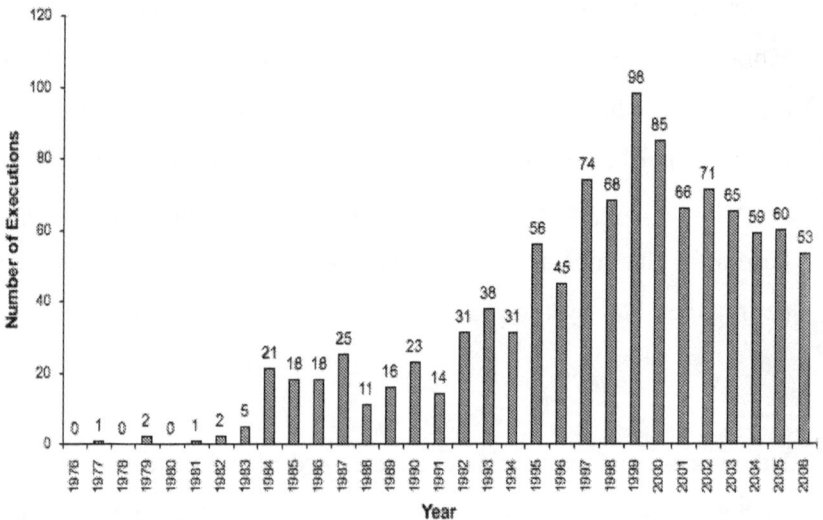

SIZE OF DEATH ROW BY YEAR

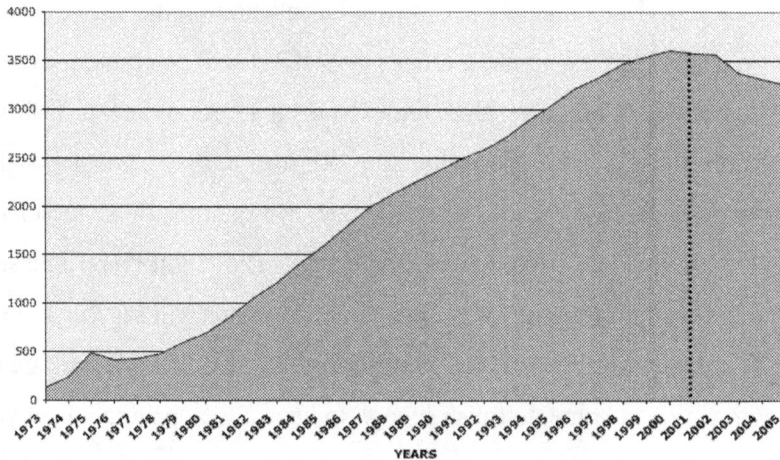

All this attention and expense on 3500 people in a country of 300 million

Well on to our next tent stake Abortion, or as the Democrats call it the Right to choose. Democrats do not want to harm a hair on the head of a convicted triple murderer but an unborn fetus is AOK! From a common sense perspective if someone is looking to have an abortion there probably is a good reason, they are too young, they are scared, they made a mistake, they will not be able to care for this child, etc. Based upon those reasons why is abortion an issue? If you do not want an abortion, don't have one seems pretty straightforward. Well the religious factions will say you are taking a life, and yes you are but for a valid reason, to not become a welfare mother, with a broken home, to finish school, to have a well paying job so you can raise a child when you are ready or mature and responsible enough to have one. People if given the choice will make the best decision, meaning if they know they are not ready for parenthood then they are not ready. To handicap your self from day one and be responsible for the life of another is a losing battle in our economic reality. While the conservatives will use the argument that people will use abortion as a form of birth control, 30 years of hard data confirms that no one is rushing out to get one simply because it trendy. The rate has leveled off even declined considering the growth of the overall population.

As detailed in Stephen Levitt's book Freakonomics there was other impacts on this particular issue. In the 1970s and early 1980s the statistics for crime showed steady growth, and the most effected by this were age groups entering adolescence and looking to express themselves. The easy path was joining with the criminals the perfect fit for the impressionable teenager with a single mother, living in the projects etc, etc. Crack dealers needed henchmen and distribution. More and more teens were becoming criminals and getting locked up every year. Crime rates were rising every year the law enforcement officials thought it was an epidemic. Then in the early 1990s something miraculous happened the crime rate started to go down, was this some great achievement of law enforcement, some incredible police strategy? No it was because of Rowe vs. Wade, 1973 which gave a woman a choice of not having a child when she was not ready which would probably go to prison on his 18th birthday and by not having that child, the mothers made the right decision. Crime rates fell because there was no crop of young impressionable teenagers to exploit and take their place in the criminal food chain. As the 1990s started the children who have been 12, and 13 and 14 if they were born did not join the criminal ranks and crime in the 1990s fell. So if you don't want an abortion don't have one, but don't tell other people what they should do.

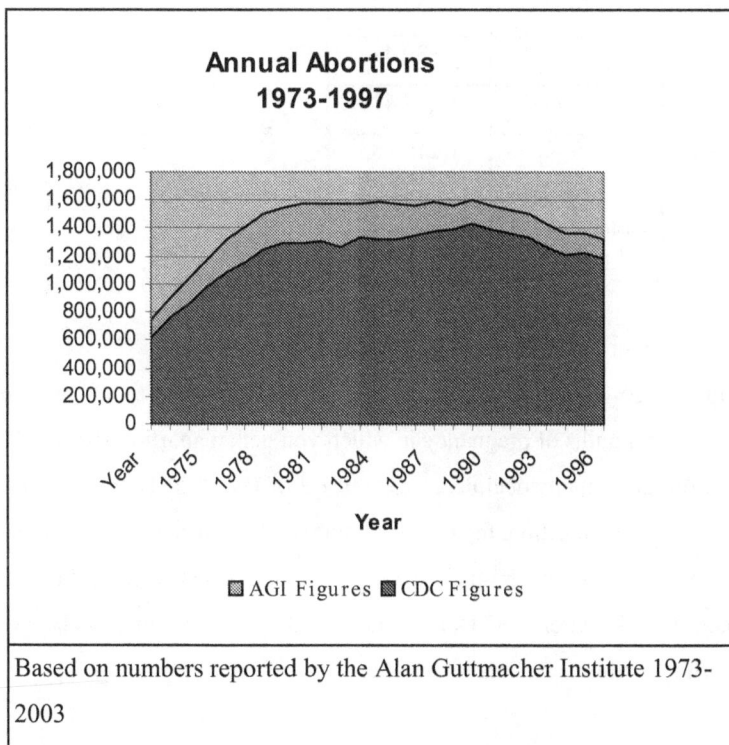

Annual Abortions 1973-1997

Based on numbers reported by the Alan Guttmacher Institute 1973-2003

Note: Data after 1997 is harder to map due to changes in reporting methods

Abortions Per Year US

1981	1,577,300	1,300,760
1982	1,573,900	1,303,980
1983	1,575,000	1,268,987
1984	1,577,200	1,333,521
1985	1,588,600	1,328,570
1986	1,574,000	1,328,112
1987	1,559,100	1,353,671
1988	1,590,800	1,371,285
1989	1,566,900	1,396,658
1990	1,608,600	1,429,247
1991	1,556,500	1,388,937
1992	1,528,900	1,359,146
1993	1,495,000	1,330,414
1994	1,423,000	1,267,415
1995	1,359,400	1,210,883
1996	1,360,160	1,225,937
1997	1,335,000	1,186,039

http://www.nrlc.org/abortion/facts/abortionstats.html

While the US Population was increasing from 250 million to 300 million and the number of months of pregnancy in which you get an abortion also increased the abortion rate actually declined, less than 1/3 of 1% of the people in our country chose to get an abortion, the rest is all drama. As you can see this is not being used as a method of contraception, the population rate is increasing and the abortion rate is not. NOTE: After 1997 Data is much harder to get because of changes in reporting methods, it is unremarkable.

Ah onto another worthless topic Gun Control, There are 90 guns for every one hundred citizens in the US, the next most armed country is India with has about 5 guns per 100 citizens. Gun control should mean the ability to hit your target but it doesn't in the political space. There are those in our country who feel that some of us should not own guns it somehow leads to crime or violence. In NYC for the past 35 years there has been a ban on all handguns in the five boroughs of NY, carrying very stiff penalties. Have you seen any lack of crime, gun crime or shootings in NYC over the last 30 years? They tried to ban guns in the UK and crime actually went up because the bad guys felt safer, they knew they had a weapon and you didn't. Now I'm not advocating the Wild West every gun I have ever seen in any state was a registered weapon. I don't think a citizen who is concerned for his self defense should be treated as a criminal. If you leave guns only in the hands of the criminal you invite crime. People always make the let the authorities' handle it case. OK , your in New Orleans and Katrina hits, or a blizzard, or landslide and you called 911 ten times no ones here, would you rather have the option of defending your home and family or would you just hope for the best? If every citizen gave up their arms only the police and military would be armed now that would be scary. Have you seen the personality profiles of the "regular" police? I'll pass on the police state, thanks. If you don't want a gun don't buy one. Then there will always be a Columbine event to make everyone crazy, those guns should have been locked up in a safe, and the parents should be tried for murder for letting the kids have access to those guns. That being said they would have found a gun somewhere else and carried out their mission because there are 200 million guns in America. Let's not let our emotions get in the way of saying the problem was with a few psychopaths not with gun control. This one really makes no difference what so ever.

GUN DATA

There are certainly reasons why you would want a firearm.

Gun-free England not such a utopia after all. According to the *BBC News*, handgun crime in the United Kingdom rose by 40% in the two years after it passed its draconian gun ban in 1997.[18] And according to a United Nations study, British citizens are more likely to become a victim of crime than are people in the United States. The 2000 report shows that the crime rate in England is higher than the crime rates of 16 other industrialized nations, including the United States.[19]

The Department of Justice found that in 1989, there were 168,881 crimes of violence which were not responded to by police within 1 hour.[47]

Former Florida Attorney General Jim Smith told Florida legislators that police responded to only about 200,000 of 700,000 calls for help to Dade County authorities.

The Pro-Gun people like to say there are over 200 million guns in America and there are, but everyone does not own a gun. Over 75% of the population does not own a gun. And only a very small minority 10 million people are "active" gun owners, this is less than 3% of the population.

NON NRA Data indicates 24% of America own guns (a gun owner owns an average of 4 guns, so despite the high number of firearms they are in a highly concentrated demographic) 80/20 rule - 10 million people actually own 105 million guns they own more than 10 guns each, most gun owners(80%+) own more than 1 gun and average 4.

Some of the Pro-Gun information is just plain nonsense.

States which passed concealed carry laws reduced their rate of murder by 8.5%, rape by 5%, aggravated assault by 7% and robbery by 3%;[29]

The gun lobby's claim here is crime reduction numbers cite reduced crime rate and rape in states that allow concealed carry of guns, but less than 9% of all gun owners are female, so this has absolutely no relevance to the reason stated, which is concealed carry of firearms. Rape is a crime against females so if only 9% of females are armed and protecting themselves against rape then 91% are not protecting themselves against rape so there is no correlation that rape rates would decrease from this minority percentage of gun ownership.

One Nation Under God, indivisible, with liberty and justice for all.

The scientific belief is that there is no god, and hence the separation of church and state, that the word god should not be in the Pledge of Allegiance. But the Pledge of Allegiance is not about science, it's a pledge, just like as if you learned a song off the radio, the original version of the pledge has the word god in it. This is no different than when they show an R-Rated movie on TV and cut out the choice words and scenes, if you go back to the original version its still there. Children learn about 3 little pigs and a wolf that don't exist, and recite starlight star bright without falling into a discussion with Nobel laureate physics majors in astronomy about whether the apparent magnitude of a star and position in the sky invalidates this claim of first star I see tonight, meaning no thought goes in to either of these little ditties so why all hung up over god. Our nation was founded on the Judea-Christian principles and religious beliefs, that we hold these truths to self evident, life, liberty and the pursuit of happiness and all that. It was a system of beliefs largely based on knowing right from wrong and trying as hard as possible to do the right thing. It has become convenient now to forget god in our hubris based upon the ivory tower thinking of separating church and state, while not even listening to the context of how it used. The word god in the pledge is used the form of patriotism and great pride with great hopes for all, not in some heaven way. Maybe we should not debate whether or not the word "god" should be permitted in the pledge of allegiance, perhaps the pledge of allegiance is passé, perhaps we should have the children read something meaningful about America that is more current like the Enron mission statement and vision. And as for the Atheists, you chose to be religion free in a country founded on religious freedoms, you are the duck out of water. No one seems to mind that our money has god written on it, not even radical Muslims or Islam-o-facsists. Whether or not you leave this word in the pledge is not a mater of national security.

Evolution

Seems there are people in our country that do not want to believe the scientific explanation of Darwin's Theory of Evolution. This is where the god word and separation of church and state come back to roost. The neo-conservatives did not like the way the Big Bang sounded a little too sexual so they came up with intelligent design theory, which means that it is possible that when a system is so complex (like the universe) that it is really hard to understand how it could have came to be you can claim it was always that way. Hey why mess with learning science if something is too hard to figure out then just say that it was always that way. "Hey Son how did this big dent get in the door of my car", well it was always there Dad. This brings us back almost to the days of Christopher Columbus saying the world was round and being jailed for it. Galileo was jailed for the about same thing. This basically is the question of faith hiding in sheep's clothing. Let them believe whatever they want at home, at family meetings, at gatherings at church, a church school, and church meetings, in public school the facts should be taught, let us not give the school system further blame for raising idiots, put raising idiots solely back into the parents hands. I for one would say change the textbooks the world is flat, and the earth is the center of universe, pigs can fly, all I would need is a shred of proof. Until then the 95,000 tons of scientific research we will have to do.

Medically Assisted Suicide

I don't know how many of you are planning medically assisted suicide so this will probably effect even less people than the four other worthless arguments above. As for me I have no wish to be a vegetable and burden to my family and healthcare system, if I was a vegetable I would want to put to death. I can not imagine other than for very selfish reasons why any family would want to keep a vegetable alive, there is no getting better. In many states suicide is illegal. Dr. Kevorkian helps people die with dignity on their own terms and he was arrested for it. It is OK if the police break down your door and shoot you, but it not OK for you to decide that you do not want to continue living with cancer and elect a medical suicide. Since we have no healthcare there is probably a piece of this puzzle still missing. Guess we are still at the sideshow.

Gay Marriage

Well here is my chance to alienate anyone that I may have missed in the first few topics. So the same group of people who are afraid to say the word god now want it to be legal for people of the same sex to marry each other. This should really only be a topic for parties of the same sex in our country who would want to be married to their partner, which in reality would be a small percentage. Unfortunately this will turn into a Sodom and Gomorrah argument for the religious right, sanctity of the family, right of a man and a woman, sacred, blah, blah, blah. Again this "big issue" is probably not going rock the boat one way or the other. What is the alternative if they can not marry continue to live together and be happy? Together. I do not think America is ready for this, while Soho and Market St. are Oh so trendy there are a few places on Brokeback mountain where this aint gonna fly. Insurance companies will hate it, financials industry will love it, retirement planning with no kids in the way, cruises and Europe

As you can see the candidates every year pretend that these are the major challenges of mankind and how they have thought of ways to insure as many people have full use of their rights in their decision making process. Then 99% they say what ever the party line is. So lets recap if you a Democrat, a liberal, you are for Right to choose , Pro choice (Abortion is OK), No Capital punishment (don't harm murders kill unborn children!!) you want More Gun control, you are afraid to say the word God in the pledge of allegiance, you like Evolution, you probably could care less about medically assisted suicide (I would say leaning towards patient choice), and you would be all for gay marriage but the other side would label you a fag loving, apocalypse creating, HIV spreading anti-Christ.

Now for the Republican, the conservatives, republicans like the death penalty they think every criminal (except those bad boys on Wall St.) should be put to death. No Abortion for you, No gun control everyone should be carrying a piece, no medically assisted suicide you can not harm the innocent, you can say God in the pledge, you can say god while you are stealing money from thy fellow man and praise god while shooting thy neighbor, No evolution here the Earth is only 6,000 years old, no gay marriage are you insane! The very gates of hell would open up.

Now while I hope my ramblings during the last few pages have kept the reader entertained you will notice that none of the topics are in the top 5 challenges in America. Not in the top 10 or top 20, that's why I call them the tent stakes of stupidity all the do is anchor part of the big top down and the more time you spend looking at the tent stakes the less time you are paying attention to something important, your looking at tent stakes nothing else. Your candidate's position on these issues is a little sideshow nothing more. What is their position on a balanced budget? Campaign finance reforms? Military Spending? Health care the full answer? Foreign Policy in the Middle East?

So while Congress has kept a minority amused it is at the expense of all of us, all these tent pegs are very small slices of the overall population, but most have a healthy big mouthed lobby. They have kept everyone occupied with the side show but the time for pacification is over it is now time solve real problems, the reason you were elected not to placate a minority of buffoons. How dare they spend the amount of time that they do on this pile of garbage? As you can clearly see there is no time for world peace and world hunger because all this bullshit is all that ever gets any play. And we need to tell the media that we have had enough, give the ratings to shows that ask candidates real questions. Because we are simply out of time for the tent stakes to play out any longer, it's like betting on number 38 on the roulette wheel, no matter where the ball lands you will still lose.

English the National Language, Nah I cant afford it

re: National Language is English

While this probably sounds like a great idea, I am holding my vote in reserve because I know the Government too well, if we made English the national language it will cost you a fortune.

First we would need a Congressional oversight committee to appoint a Director for the program. The director would get a budget and a staff and he would need to promote English as a National Language, he would hire a staff and need a building, phones, computers etc. He would probably set up a general manager to run the program in each state, they would need a staff, then each State would need a liaison to its federal counterpart, are you following me here? By the end of the year we would have 6,995 people on the payroll who speak English. Added cost to you (50 states x 100 employees + 50 state x 20 employees + HQ staff) 7000 employees x $40K average (rent, salaries, benefits, soc sec, etc) $280,000,000.00 yearly

You'll like this one even better. So now that we have a National language the Government would be obligated to print the official English language dictionary (Or pay Webster's to do it) and a program on learning English for immigrants, these would be huge books, and multiple volumes, English is a very complex language. Someone in the Senate who is sucking up because he needs votes would stand up and say "We should give each and every one of the 12 Million illegal aliens these official books free of charge so they can learn the national language if they want to become integrated into our society", hell since it is a government document they would probably have to provide it for anyone that asked for it. Someone else would say what a great idea that was and the program would go into law. They would then realize that there are 40 million illegal immigrants NOT 12 million, people will lose books and request a second copy, every library and school, public place, University would want a set of these books. English usage changes all the time so there would need to be updates at least yearly, and immigrant families may want a copy for each of their 4 or 5 kids and send a few back home for some relatives who aspire to come here, people move and lose the books they call the free 800 number and order more. (I need a staff to man the phones and take the orders oh and a web site and email requests) By the way you would also need to publish the book in at least the top 30 languages at additional cost. 100M copies per year x $5-10 per books + shipping $500,000,000 yearly

We would then need TV advertisement and an Ad campaign to promote speaking English (tell me I don't know Uncle Sam), "Just say No", "Take a bite out of crime" and "Just speak English", and we could subsidize companies that use English as their language. And a cool superhero for the kids to look up to , like Captain English-O with a spot at the halftime show at the Superbowl, yearly cost to you $90,000,000. Did I mention the T-shirts?

I would not mind the cost but I am still paying off the Saving and Loan bailout, the Star Wars program, 3 Mile Island, Love Canal, The 1st Gulf War, the 2nd Iraqi War, .70c per gallon for gas, a New-New Orleans oh and a Superdome with a new seawall thrown in so I don't have much left for this "English program" sorry.

DESTROYING AMERICA

Chapter 11 - American Health (non) Care

The Healthcare issues in America can a very complex topic. I think before we start it is important to recognize one of the main drawbacks of the existing "system". 50 million Americans, 1 in 6 people not having healthcare coverage puts a higher cost on everyone who does have coverage. The current system also puts the insurance companies (payers) in control of our healthcare system. Doctors go to school for about 10 years so they can become Doctors, they do this in order to be qualified to practice medicine and provide care, and then they also must pass stringent tests in order to practice medicine. But the doctors, who are licensed and qualified to practice medicine do not run the health care system, they are simply a vendor, submitting bills to a big machine, and submitting bills on the big machines terms and on the proper color paper, the color paper that the big machine likes that month. How did we ever allow our system of healthcare to be run by accountants, actuaries and statisticians? If you broke your hand at a picnic would you run down to your accountant's office? Of course you wouldn't. These people manage risk, but they do not have a degree in medicine. If you were to ask an accountant any question regarding spending money and the answer will be no, this is not someone who should be determining whether you live or die and controlling healthcare costs. An accountant is not qualified to be a Doctor and should not decide what you do or do not need in terms of your health.

Number 2, in the current system the insurance carriers have pretty much formed a monopoly and there is absolutely no competition. The first principle of economics is the law of supply and demand with a monopoly in place none of the benefits of capitalism, i.e. competition, can function properly. When there is marketplace competition prices remain in check, when there is no competition there are runaway prices, as in the case of healthcare in general, healthcare costs and prescription medicine. In any other market where there is competition whether there are increases or fluctuations the competition keeps the price fluctuations minimized this is the nature of competition. With no competition, I can charge whatever I want for services, I charge whatever I want and charge you back for it. We have seen the case where an insured person goes to the doctor and the office visit costs $120. The doctor collects the patient's co-payment, let us say $10, and then bills the insurance company for the rest.

But the insurance company pays the doctor an agreed upon rate usually $70 for a doctors visit, and the insurance company tells you that you received a $120 of benefits, based upon their buying power and $10 out of your pocket. But the Health insurance companies are in the 30-40%-50% profit margin and even more just for passing paper. Having a middleman like this in this model with these exorbitant fees does not make economic sense. This would be the equivalent of you buying something in the real world for $1,000 and MasterCard expecting a $400 fee from you for the convenience of using their card. Since all this stuff is hidden in the secret world of insurance you do not get to see how ridiculous it is. I know this is America and we all have to make a profit to stay in business, but when we are talking about healthcare and keeping people alive and healthy a 40% premium does seem a bit egregious, especially if we are talking about a matter of life and death.

Moreover these organizations add no value to the process; they only control it and drive the costs up to suit Wall Street expectations. The doctors and hospitals are not making more money the healthcare insurers are. The wrong people are profiting form the system, this incents no one. The government could very easily put a few measures in effect to force these companies to compete and bring about market equilibrium. The government could institute incentives and rebates and creating ceilings, standards and floors along with tax breaks. The government could do this, but they don't because of the number of representatives who are on the take for maintaining the status quo on this sorry excuse of a system, a broken system where an accountant decides if you need an operation. Real competition keeps prices down look at phone service versus the price of gasoline over the last 10 years.

Let me outline in the first sentence here what I am not advocating, we do not want socialized medicine in the form of government run healthcare, we do not want another Post Office-like organization with the word health care on it. What we do want is a private company, which is run really well like a FedEx or UPS (since I used the post office as an example) to oversee the program within the federal guidelines. Preferably a well run company that already does this on a daily basis, they can be the administrator of the plan, a firm like a Blue Shield, Aetna, United Health, Kaiser or a similar, but with new guidelines. The existing Healthcare payee system is already set up and it works, it simply needs to be retooled so that we are not overcharging people and making exorbitant profits. They can make a fair fee for services but not 40%. Hey, once the US government gets involved you can be sure there will be no profit. This should be just like private healthcare with the regular doctor you already have the only difference will be where the payment check may actually come from. People have different ideas when general terms like "Universal Health Care" or "socialized medicine", "National Healthcare". This would be no different than something you would sign up for yourself today, if you called Blue Shield, and signed up for a plan and you go see your own doctors; this is more like a giant PPO (Preferred Provider Organization, go see any doctor) or HMO (Health Maintenance Organization, more like a certain medical network, with the ability to go out of network) with more options. Just like when you have a car accident and you go to the body work shop of your choice, if you are part of the Government "system" the Government may be either a partial payer the payer, but they may not be the administrator of the system because they are not very good at it. We do not want to create a new division of government bureaucracy to deal with something which they have no expertise in.

For those who are scared of the words government healthcare let me give you a baseline so you do not run away. Think of the government plan like being a member of Costco, they buy in bulk and they have a special rate that you could not get on your own. You take advantage of that buying power, just like at Sam's Club, Wal-Mart, BJ's and Costco. If you try to get family health coverage or small business health coverage you know these plans can be very costly. But huge companies like AT&T, IBM, Exxon, GM, Microsoft, Proctor and Gamble, BP, Coke, Citigroup, GE, Sony, HP, Dell, any many more, negotiate based upon the number of employees and even though health costs are rising these companies manage to put together attractive health benefits packages for their employees and keep the costs down. Now picture if these companies all banded together to get an even better rate with more buying power from their healthcare provider, and then imagine if they offered this to you at Costco. You do not have to be an employee, you sign up for the year and pay $200 per month and for a family of four, for full coverage! If you followed me so far just swap the name from Costco to US Government Health Plan and rely on the buying power to get a better premium. That is the premise, "US Government Health Plan" in name only. This is not government doctors, and government hospitals and facilities, and government testing labs, it is all private practitioners with the existing coverage guidelines, only where the money comes from will change. So, sorry you will not going to the Post Office for your measles shot or the DMV for a rectal exam, but you may get one anyway.

We may also want to redefine what we call it. Because insurance has such a negative connotation; and for good reason. You purchase life insurance so if you die your family receives a payment for your death. We have car insurance in case something happens to our car but if something does happen to our car the insurance company will fix the car but they will also jack up your rates. Perhaps the right word for this would be "coverage" as opposed to insurance because you should use your coverage all the time and not be penalized for it. Going to the doctor has to lose the stigma of being a bad thing as well. Your are covered for using the healthcare system, which would include a yearly physical to help keep you healthy, along with doctor visits, medicine, tests, specialists, surgery etc.

There are several workable healthcare plans from various candidates, some are fairly similar and from the general summaries look great, we do need to look at the details, weigh the pros and cons. And while I am not a Hillary Clinton fan I will recognize her plan, the work she put in to it and give it a slight nod. John Edwards says his plan is very similar and does not "pander" to special interests, I am not taking sides, the goal here is to have a workable real solution. (I am also not being partisan here but all I have seen from the Republican candidates are the plans for war, health care is someone else's problem) Clinton took the lumps and bruises 12 years ago with the first go around for a National Healthcare referendum, she has also had the last 12 years to learn firsthand from her mistakes and to gain insight from the best minds in our country on what a good plan needs to succeed, what it was missing, what it must have and how to make it work. So in this area I think she is 12 years ahead of many others on this subject and she does not need to be President in order to bring about the changes, it could be a new cabinet position, or a simply a house committee to deploy a healthcare plan. It does not necessarily need to be her plan verbatim, but I think capitalizing on her true experience in this area would be a smart move for our country. What we should do is take the best parts from several plans and cobble them together that's what makes a America great, don't continuously reinvent the wheel. None of us has all the answers but there is no shortage of great minds in our country, and I truly feel that if you lock a dozen or so qualified experts in a room for the week you could get an 80% improvement on the issues.

"Well doesn't Canada have this socialized medicine thing; I heard there are lines and people had to wait." We have all heard the bad things and rumors that the American Insurance companies and drug companies, and all the organizations that are making the most profits like to scare you with. People wait in line at the mall for useless crap, they wait in line at the toll booth on the bridge, they wait in line at Starbucks and the Latte is not going to save your life. Let me reiterate, if you have your own healthcare and like it, then this does not affect you. Or if you do not like your existing coverage you will now have a choice which you currently do not have. Now for the other 50+ million people who have NO coverage, if you had to wait in line to see a doctor would that be such a bad thing? Their current option is to do nothing, so if you have no coverage and no doctor, then no line for you, stay home and be sick. This is a lot like saying you want filet mignon but you are really, really hungry and a peanut butter and jelly sandwich is starting to sound pretty good. I would go so far as to say that waiting in a line would beat dying. Other highly advanced civilized nations have similar systems, and nothing is going to perfect and we are all going to need time to adapt and change. But lets not pretend that what we have is some kind of Nirvana, it is not, and for 20% of our citizens they have garbage, they have nothing, and this is driving up the costs on those that have coverage. We are all in this together like it or not. If you like your current coverage, I will hasten a guess that you would like your plan even more if it would stop costing 15% more each year.

By providing an alternative healthcare plan your healthcare costs will stabilize, and by providing the uninsured coverage there are no surprise costs in the system to jump the prices up so rapidly, the costs of healthcare to everyone will be less volatile and more stable. Having coverage also helps to prevent the "Big unexpected expense", the stroke or heart attack, with a triple bypass, when the person has no coverage they wait until catastrophe strikes and gets put in an ambulance; this is our current system, wait until you are on fire then run for the hose. Again this is going to take time to get accustomed to and make adjustments. A major "catastrophic illness" is also the second highest cause of bankruptcy each year in our country. If everyone had coverage for an annual check up hopefully for a majority of people the problems would be caught well before the heart attack. People now do not have to wait for the ambulance in order to see a doctor.

We can also look at the Canadians, Germans and French and other countries and other ideas and identify specifically what is working well and what we should avoid, no system will ever be perfect. What we also need to recognize it that the number #1 thing we need to do about our health in the US is called prevention. This health tip coming from a country where Approximately 127 million adults in the U.S. are overweight, 60 million obese, and 9 million severely obese. In 2006, only four states had a prevalence of obesity less than 20%. Twenty-two states had a prevalence equal or greater than 25%; two of these states (Mississippi and West Virginia) had a prevalence of obesity equal to or greater than 30%. http://www.cdc.gov/nccdphp/dnpa/obesity/trend/maps/   Basically this means 1 in 4 of us walking around daily in the United States is close to or over 20-25 lbs overweight, diet and exercise is a much needed component of "healthcare" and the future depends on it. The trend continues the number of obese adults continues to increase every year while 64% of adults in the United States over the age of 21 are considered overweight. In 1998 "Treatment for Obesity" was 9.1% of the total costs included in total medical expenditures, at approximately $51 Billion dollars (not including economic loss).

But this is just the tip of the iceberg as chronic obesity can lead to multiple other health related issues including: hypertension, Osteoarthritis, Dyslipidemia, Type 2 diabetes, Coronary heart disease, Heart Attack, Stroke, Gallbladder disease, Sleep Apnea, some cancers (endometrial, breast, colon etc,) the treatment for these conditions does not fall under obesity, but obesity is often the cause. At this rate this will be 20-30% of our citizens will already have built-in health related problems because of being overweight. Part of the problem is that America companies can still call a box of lard and sugar "food", or even a "healthy snack" if they like. But this is not to put the blame solely on the companies there is plenty of garbage out there to eat but ultimately it is our fault for eating it, we are the ones who do not say no, I can not eat this its not food. We know that Ding-Dongs, Twinkies and Doritos are not food and blaming McDonalds is not the answer. This is both a huge future problem health wise for our country as well as a potentially costly one down the road. Any healthcare plan must have a diet and exercise component or ultimately it will fail. We must provide information and education so that people can make the right choices for diet and exercise, awareness is key.

Another thing we are not doing right. Prescription drug use in the United States has gone up 100% in the past decade. The primary reasons for this are the $9 Billion dollars in advertising that the drug companies spend each year, telling you that you need drugs. The pharmaceutical companies are spending as much money as Coke and Pepsi to drive a message into your brain that you need their products, just ask your doctor. If you needed a drug to help you chances are the doctor would be telling you about it, not vice versa. American medicine treats the symptoms not the problem so prescribing drugs is an easy fix for everybody and a cash cow, but ultimately we will be overpaying for it. Unnecessary prescriptions do not help anyone, except the profit margin for the pharmaceutical companies. There is also no reason why you should not be able to buy your prescription from Canada or Mexico where they are half price, and the government can force the price correction.

The RAND Corporation and some other very well known think tanks put annual savings in the $60-$120-$165 Billion dollars, this represents a 10% reduction in overall healthcare costs while insuring 20% more people, and giving more people more choices and options for healthcare. This will also stabilize healthcare prices, give coverage to 100% of the country and slow the rate of price increases on healthcare.

DESTROYING AMERICA

Chapter 12 – Immigration

Immigration and illegal immigration are probably to most complex topics to address because there definitely is no easy answer and any course of action will have serious economic and social consequences. Because of the implications the immigration issue has avoided whenever possible by elected officials and only paid lip service and that is why it has grown into such a serious problem with massive proportions. It is also a difficult subject because of our American heritage, the great melting pot, everyone here now at one time had parents or grandparent that emigrated here in the past. They all came from somewhere else. They came to make a better life, to give the families a better life, and this melting pot is what made America the "greatest country in the world", and the Statue of Liberty proclaims the tradition to give us "your tired, your poor, your huddled masses". Many American families can proudly trace their family tree all the way back to Ellis Island. So now our citizens denying this same opportunity to others can seem hypocritical or even the politically incorrect phrase of racist.

Second, let me define separate issues within the broad topic of "Immigration" There is a legal and normal process for immigration, which it is in dire need of overhaul, it is not working. A sub-issue within legal immigration is one for highly-skilled technical workers, such as software engineers who can get a temporary visa known as an H-1B visa based upon their specialized knowledge this process has created more problems than it solved. The next issue is illegal immigration, such as people walking across the border; this is usually what people mean when they think about the "immigration" problem. This illegal immigration is the primary issue. Within the illegal immigration problem there is a very specific problem with Mexico because of the geography between our two countries. The Mexican problem is a very large problem because of the massive amount of people coming across the border. To put this in perspective; the US only admits about 1 million legal aliens through the normal immigration process per year, while the Border patrol made 1.1 million arrests alone in 2004. By the Border Patrol estimates they stopped about 10% of the people crossing the border, is could be more or less they have no way to know. The Border patrol believes that between 4-10 million people cross the border from Mexico every year, some they catch, some return to Mexico, some do not. Quantities like this are completely out of proportion to having a sustainable legal immigration process. So specifically there are illegal immigration problems and clearly there is a Mexican illegal immigration problem and if that is racist then so be it.

We are not the first generation to face a problem with immigrants. At the turn of the 20th century the English and Dutch citizens who were in the initial waves of people who settled in the new world were concerned with the amounts of the Irish immigrants coming to America. They were concerned about crime, and where they were going to live, and losing jobs to these new immigrants. The new immigrants took the lower paying more difficult jobs that nobody else wanted worked hard and eventually proved themselves as able people and hard workers, with some reluctance they were by a large accepted into society. The next wave of immigrants that concerned the public then became the Italians, with concerns over the same issues of crime, resources, and losing jobs again these new immigrants took the lowest jobs on the ladder and worked hard to be accepted and the story continues through today. The difference is in the past is that manageable quantities of people came to America and were able to assimilate and contribute to society. While the Whitehouse and Congress are afraid to label what is going on with Mexico, 4 to 10 million people crossing our border in wartime would qualify as an invasion and in peacetime a more apt word may be epidemic. While the border with Mexico is not the only immigration problem it a gushing head wound and without treatment will lead to a host other problems and it already is a source of many problems costing over $200 Billion dollars per year.

For those of you who do not live near the border or a major metropolitan area some of these discussions may seem unnecessary the simple answer of "send them back" may seem the right thing to do, and an obvious answer but unfortunately it is not just that simple. Some of these workers include, doctors, nurses, software developers, and scientist's not just people who pick tomatoes. I will try to put some background into this subject before continuing. There are many problems with our normal immigration process but the major issues are with illegal immigration in our country.

The current group of politicians throws around various buzzwords, such as: "amnesty", "day worker", "day labor" "temporary worker", "guest worker", "undocumented worker" and various other similar phrases, none of these words is actually an answer to anything, only a different way to define the problem. Since none of these terms address the problem I will not spend any more time on any of them. The politicians continue to use the number of 11 million illegal immigrants, because they extrapolated this number from the

US census data, since an illegal immigrant by definition would not want to be counted in a census I do not know how the census could have any relevance in knowing how many illegal immigrants are living in the US, since they would not be included in any US Census data. Later in this chapter I will detail why this number is incorrect as for this part of the discussion I will use the 11 million illegal aliens number from the government, but only as a reference or bookmark. The politicians also seem to pretend that somehow these 11 million illegal aliens snuck across the border in the middle of the night just last weekend, and we just do not know what to do with them. Obviously this is not the case it is convenient to pretend that this just became a problem.

The Democrats like illegal aliens because historically lower income people favor the Democratic Party because of their embrace with social programs. So the democrats see future voters, democrats also want to endear themselves to this economic group they send the message to current voters with lower incomes who interact daily with illegal aliens that they understand the lower income voter and they are the candidate who cares and who can help the voter. Republicans are a lot simpler they see cheap, plentiful labor, no unions, no medical care, this keeps prices down for the consumer, it helps the companies who employ illegal aliens make more money without raising prices. While no one from either party is going to run forward and proclaim that these are the reasons why they do nothing about immigration, ask to see what they have done, and you will see nothing.

People talk about the cost to society and there is significant cost but lets look at the economic impact. When crops are ripe the farmers really do need workers people in urban areas may not be very familiar with this. Farms need workers not lengthy administration processes. An illegal worker who will work for $10 per hour costs 40% less than his Californian counterpart because of Social Security, State Taxes, Disability, Medicare, etc, so the native worker costs $14 per hour, a 40% premium, he picks the same amount of lettuce and strawberries as his illegal counterpart. For a full time employee if you add medical, retirement, and a vacation, you are easily in the $17 to $20 range for a $10 per hour employee. Sooner or later all these costs are passed on to you, if a farms labor price doubled then the cost per head of lettuce, per bushel of corn, or per pint of strawberries will go up by some percent, maybe 2-5% this is at the wholesale level. The distributor passes his cost increase on to the supermarket chains, adding another 10% and the supermarkets pass it on to you, adding another 10%. The restaurants pass it on to you, McDonalds, frozen food maker, with higher prices. A 1% or 2% price increase in the cost of food after the ripple effect can be tens of billions of dollars. So the farming industry loves cheap labor, fast food outlets, supermarkets all love cheap labor and it keeps the CPI index down so the government statisticians love it too, but they can put that in a press release. But the side benefit is that poor people can afford more food.

Food accounted for 10% of domestic GDP so the economic impact of a price increase on just food will have an impact on a $1.3 Trillion dollar portion of GDP, plus associated restaurant services, supermarkets, goods and related industries. Bear in mind that this is one industry but there are many others that use illegal aliens for labor such as hotels, construction, labor, landscaping, janitorial, restaurants, and retail as well which will have a similar end result. This could easily be $100 billion dollars in price increases passed on to you. This is not the only economic impact. If we take the case of the worker above each worker who works for $10 per hour is displacing a worker for almost $20 per hour. This will equate to earnings of about $20,000 per year per illegal alien, rather than the $40,000 earning for the citizen worker at the full burden rate at the same time the illegal alien may be paying no taxes on any of these earnings. In essence this non payment of $20,000 in additional wages, benefits, mandatory state and federal costs to 11 million people which equates to American farm industry avoiding a $220 Billion dollar cost. This cost would also be passed on to you. But this also helps keep wages down for all lower paying jobs. If we do something really radical like deport everyone the result could be a $75 pint of strawberries, or $50 head of lettuce and a 20-30% vacancy rate on rental apartments throughout the southwest, and no cabbies in NYC, no hotel workers in Las Vegas it looks good on paper to "send them all back" but it does not work that way. While this is an exaggeration you can see the impact it would have.

Many people do not understand the economic upside that we gain from this "cheap" labor they only know of the costs of illegal aliens when they see something negative flashed on the news. Most of the illegal aliens work very hard at strenuous jobs and make very little money; they are outgoing, honest and reliable workers. So let's put another piece into the puzzle because it is not all their fault, when they got here no one told them to go back, as a matter of fact we welcomed them with open arms. As I mentioned previously did no one notice this "problem" when it was say 1 million people, 2 million, 3 million people, then over night 11 million people just appeared? The realtors did not know they were renting to "illegal's", the Gas and Electric companies, did not know they were providing service to "illegal's" the Phone, and Cable companies did not know these buyers were "illegal", the credit card companies did not know?, how do you get a credit card without a social security number? How did the banks open an account without proper identification? The US banks did not know? Nobody knew. A big mystery of where 11 million people just appeared. You see even though the illegal's make very little money all the American companies lined up to take their cut, lower income people always wind up paying the most in banking fees because they do not have many deposits same with credit cards every else wants their money too.

So if you are here illegally and you are provided phone and cable TV and Credit cards and banking services wouldn't you start to think that you maybe did not have to leave, America wants me here or I would not have all these things. No one in the supermarket or at Wal-Mart is saying I'm sorry I can not let you buy that without ID, we all take whatever little money they have. Roy Beck pointed out numerous immigration problems in his "By the Numbers" book and documentary 10 years ago. (www.numbersusa.com), The Government has done nothing because they want to pretend that our healthy economy and GDP is growing at 2-3% (GDP) annually and secretly they rely on the immigrants to "need" all the necessities of life when they get here, towels, rugs, sheets, pillows, beds, toilet paper, TVs, furniture, soap, everything etc, etc, etc, all these little purchases make the economy look like it is growing when in fact it is not, because the very people doing the buying are not even counted in the equation those clever little government math statisticians! (Took a lesson from the Enron School of math) And all those extra little purchases in the consumer goods column are just enough to push us over the top on paper and show the world our economic strength! Much of our growth is on the backs of people who should not be living here but don't tell anyone. A couple million people sneaking over and setting up shop here makes our financial balance sheet a little nicer that's why no one has done nor will do anything about it, besides the "cheap" labor keeps inflation and prices down (CPI), no politician has touched touch issue this with a 10 foot pole.

Now to dispel the infamous 11 million illegal alien statistic.
San Diego County remittances to Mexico hit $1.1 Billion   Union Tribune Newspaper October 19 2007 "The amount of money the workers in San Diego County send to Mexico has ballooned to $1.1 Billion dollars from $800 Million in 2004 according to the World bank. .. The bulk of $24.2 billion sent to Mexico last year almost $13 Billion came from California."

First statistical method
Still think there are 11 million immigrants in the whole country?   So if there were 1 million illegal immigrants in California that would mean that every single one of them sent home $13,000 dollars Every single alien sent home $13,000. Every single one. But at $10 per hour (some earn far less) they would make $20,800 a year assuming they worked steadily for 5 days a week, and paid their rent and food with less than $600 per month? I don't think every single immigrant sent home almost 65% of their pay or they could not afford to stay in California, now if every immigrant sent home $200 per month or even $400 per month that would be 2.6 million people, but do you think "every" immigrant is sending home $5,000 per year or say 1 out of 3 or 4 immigrants are, that would make 10.4 million illegal immigrants in California alone. Based upon the facts from the World Bank numbers, California is 1 state out of 50; Mexico is 1 country out of 300. So that would be 10.4 million illegal aliens in California based upon the World Bank facts.

Number 2, we have the entire money trail and the banking tracked down to the penny still think there is no way to stop this problem? What would be a reason why we would not stop this and solve this "illegal" alien's problem? The banking fees for wire transfers on deposits of $13 Billion dollars is $75 million dollars per year, the bank earns the overnight funds rate on these deposits which is another $65 million and the banks make another $100 million on loans during the year while the money is "in process", $240 million reasons why "we can do anything about this" this is money from just one state. Migrants sent home funds totaling $300 Billion dollars last year (World Bank) you do the math and tell me who benefited.

Second statistical method

Regarding this latest Mexico protests in June 2007 it is hilarious, they closed all the high schools for 2 or 3 days in San Diego and Los Angeles because the schools were 70-85% empty . Apparently 70-85% of the high school students and other schools are children from illegal aliens so the schools which they are not paying for are empty during the protest. Another way to look at this is when the illegal alien children are in school and not protesting my tax dollars are educating people who should NOT be in the country in the first place, you cant make this stuff up, I wonder what 3-4 high schools, teachers, lunches, buses, etc are costing us? So now conservatively if illegal alien children account for 65% of the kids, assuming 2 children per family, then that makes illegal aliens roughly 35% of the population (and Uncounted), (and these are the kids enrolled in school, not the ones staying home) there are 30 million census counted people in CA, illegal aliens do not want to be counted, 35% of 30M is 11M and that is California only. So you do the math for the rest of America and see what you think. We could close 65% of the schools if we did not educate illegal aliens, that would be a 65% cost reduction. We realize they have no other way to show their voices but not going to school which is provided to you free is not the brightest idea.

In fairness I have a question for the protesters: I want to know if I drive my family down to Mexico and rent a house can my kids show up at school and take lessons (without cost)? Can I get a job in Mexico? Can I vote in Mexico? Can I buy real estate in Mexico? Can I become a Mexican citizen? (If I was say 12 years old) Can I walk into a high school in Canada or Mexico and take Biology on the house? If I went to Jamaica for the winter can my kids go to school for free there?

A third common sense and un-statistical method for the number of illegal aliens would be, if you ever lived or spent time in the NYC metro area, Los Angeles metro, Dallas, Las Vegas, the border areas of Arizona, New Mexico and California, the farm areas of California, Florida, Texas just by using your senses you would quickly notice that about 10% of the population are illegal aliens, certainly not every illegal alien is from Mexico. From experience in NYC region I would easily estimate 10 million illegal aliens in the greater NYC area alone. There are 300 million people in the US so 10% would be 30 million people but this is less scientific than using numbers from the World Bank.

We have an obligation to provide life, liberty, and the pursuit of happiness, the bill of rights and as much opportunity as we can to our citizens, not to the entire world and while it may be unfortunate we can not take every person in the world who has less than we do under our wing, that is just reality.

Now let's look at some not so good statistics that come along with the illegal alien problem. There is a mid size town in Arizona very close to the border called Yuma. Yuma Arizona has a population of about 80,000 people and about 150,000 in total in the surrounding county area. In 2003-2005 the average total number of aliens who were caught crossing the border in the Yuma/Tucson area was over 300,000 people. The Yuma portion of these aliens was about 120,000-140,000 illegal aliens per year. Imagine the burden, the manpower and resources used by a small town in processing 12,000 illegal aliens per month; this is 400 people per day. Many people are against the Mexican wall for good reason it does set us back 200 years, but this situation with Mexico has not improved in the last 15 years, and their President encourages this type of activity, so doing nothing has not worked so a wall may at least slow the onslaught. Of the 1.1 million illegal aliens caught last year 98% of them came through the southern border areas. There are 12,000 government employees in Yuma so what do you think all this cost us annually? Along with the 300,000 illegal aliens 300,000 lbs of marijuana was also stopped with the aliens. Entire school districts are popping up in Arizona where there are very few kids according to the census numbers. The Mexico wall really is a last resort, but they left us no choice. Bush approved $2.2 Billion dollars for 700 mile wall; Homeland Security promised 70 miles would be built in 18 months, but after the first 12 months less than 15 miles was actually built so apparently this was an election year gimmick. One would imagine that we would have the technology and know how to build a fence. Fences make good neighbors. Even it is finished we still have 95,000 miles of coastline. The Mexican government also said that they would not allow the US to build a wall as if they had a say in the matter. So how does Mexico deal with their neighbors? They build a wall take a look at Mexico's southern border it is a completely militarized crossing, fence, troops, guns, and tanks.

Here are the major costs for Illegal Aliens:

1. $11 Billion to $22 billion is spent on welfare to illegal Aliens

2. $2.2 Billion dollars a year is spent on food assistance Programs such as food stamps, WIC, and free school lunches for illegal Aliens.

3. $2.5 Billion dollars a year is spent on Medicaid for illegal Aliens.

4. $12 Billion dollars a year is spent on primary and secondary School education for children here illegally and they cannot speak a word of English.

5. $17 Billion dollars a year is spent for education for the American-born children of illegal aliens, known as anchor babies.

6. $3 Million Dollars a DAY is spent to incarcerate illegal Aliens.

7. 30% percent of all Federal Prison inmates are illegal aliens. (this is correct but the data is skewed because border crossing is a federal offense)

8. $90 Billion Dollars a year is spent on illegal aliens for Welfare & social services by the American taxpayers.

9. $200 Billion Dollars a year in suppressed American wages are Caused by the illegal aliens. (possibly)

10. The illegal aliens in the United States have a crime rate that's two and a half times that of white non-illegal aliens. In particular, Their children, are going to make a huge additional crime problem in the US.

11. During the year of 2005 there were 4 to 10 MILLION illegal Aliens that crossed our Southern Border also, as many as 19,500 illegal Aliens from Terrorist Countries. Millions of pounds of drugs, cocaine, meth, Heroine and marijuana, crossed into the U. S from the Southern border. Ref: Homeland Security.

12. The National Policy Institute, "estimated that the total Cost of mass deportation would be between $206 and $230 billion or an Average cost of between $41 and $46 billion annually over a five year Period."

13. In 2006 illegal aliens sent home $45 BILLION in remittances back to their countries of origin.

14. "The Dark Side of Illegal Immigration: Nearly One Million Sex Crimes Committed by Illegal Immigrants In The United States ".

The total economic impact is $338.3 Billion dollars per year
Even without suppressed wages there is over a $150 Billion dollar price tag here, which we pay.

When you take the good news and the bad news and mix in the fact that most of these people are just good, hard working people many of us just throw up their hands because it is very convoluted issue and it is. But there certainly are things the government can do while I am not a fan of police state measures I think having 30 to 40 million people here who are not paying taxes are adding to everyone's burden and they are growing to a majority amount to an invasion. Many of these problems date back to Supreme Court decision that say you can not deny someone emergency room care and somehow that got translated into you can not deny someone an education.

We could simply pass a law that would not allow purchases at any store without a valid driver's license, same with utilities, phone, etc. No drivers license no purchases. Then No proper documentation no bank account, existing accounts have 90 days to clear up their records. With big fines for the banks, Wal-Mart, Target and anyone else who messes around with this.

We could institute huge fines and jail time for any business using illegal aliens, if there was no work for them they would go home. We could outlaw money transfers to Mexico, or better yet withhold 50% for taxes, and confiscate 50% at the border, if you do not file a tax return we keep it. We are very far from the there's nothing you can do type answers.

Where these illegal aliens have clearly crossed the line, besides crossing the border is in their protests where they now "demand" a path to citizenship it has simply gone too far. They wave their countries flags and are dictating to our government and to us what they want, but they should not want anything from our government they should not be here. They pay no taxes and their children get a free education, and if they walk into a hospital they get free healthcare so overall they got a pretty good deal, while they make less money they get some good fringe benefits. Again turnabout is fairplay what do you think would happen to us if 1 million of us marched down to Mexico City and had a public protest and demanded citizenship? If we did not get shot, we certainly would wind up in jail, and we would not be innocent until proven guilty in a Mexican jail.

I am a realist I think that we will simply grant "amnesty" (or whatever you want to call it) to the 30 million that are here, it would be easier and then they would have to pay taxes, I do not think this is the right thing to do but it is realistic. What I do want is to prevent the next 40 million from coming and repeating the process.

DESTROYING AMERICA

Chapter 13 - Hydrogen Fuel: The Big Lie

Sorry citizens of the United States but there is no Santa Claus

I hate to be the one to have to break the news and point out things like: the Easter bunny is fake, there is no tooth fairy or Santa Claus is dead. But Hydrogen Fuel being "the solution" for our cars is a complete bullshit story. Bush gave $1.7B for hydrogen research in 2007 and GM was glad to scarp that money up, like throwing a lifeline to a drowning man. But the reality is, hydrogen is a long, long way from prime time. So far away it is a joke on the American people. The fact it is even being mentioned in the mainstream as a possible solution is ridiculous, we are about as close to having a usable, realistic, economic Hydrogen solution as we are to making Transporters from Star Trek which would eliminate cars altogether.

But there are a litany of reasons why experts tout the benefits of hydrogen. A few of the main reasons why hydrogen is being touted as the "solution", for getting off oil, pollution, global warming, fossil fuel elimination etc.

1) It makes everyone happy, the only emissions are water vapor it is a tree huggers wet dream. Something the Sierra club and Greenpeace can not even bitch about. Politicians like it, car makers, consumers, researchers like it what a great idea! No pollution, no C2O, no global warming, rainbows everywhere, sunshine, ice cream, happy, happy, rainbows and puppies!

2) The promise of this technology is just beyond our reach, its right around

the corner, if you can just be patient it will be a brighter tomorrow. It currently does not exist but there's been promising research and….. The oil companies love this reason, you are stuck for the next 10-15 years which becomes 20-25 yrs all the time they make $6 Billion dollars per day in the US alone, they WANT you on oil for another 15 years, The Government loves this too no one has to make a decision or have any vision or leadership it is a nice 15 year hiatus from having to take action. "somebody else's problem". Car companies love it too, why change anything when you can ram the same crap down your throat with a different number (07, 08, 09, 2010, 2011) stamped on it. Why invent anything, why innovate? No matter how you tried you could not implement this tomorrow its not ready anyway. AND its guilt free for the consumer too, no thinking no choices we have to wait until this hydrogen stuff is ready that's all we can do.

3) No infrastructure exists that can carry hydrogen nationally, nor are there enough production facilities, pipelines. Holding tanks etc, and it is a very specialized gas needs to be highly pressurized, none of these things exist and will need to be built costing trillions of dollars.

4) Very Important: to go 500 miles in a Hydrogen car right now the current process to make hydrogen would use more fossil fuels through electricity in creating the Hydrogen than just using gasoline. This is worth repeating we actually use more fossil fuels creating hydrogen right now then if you just used the fossil fuels so currently it is not smart alternative.. But they are improving the efficiency of this method.
Right now there is NO savings of fossil fuel or pollution in the creation of Hydrogen

This would deter 99% of scientists but not the US Government! There is no where on our planet where hydrogen is sitting waiting to be collected. The process to get hydrogen from water uses a lot of electricity or it comes from fossil fuel, creating about the same amount of pollution.

5) Lastly and most important you can not make hydrogen yourself, so invariably after 20 years of jerking around you will trade your oil addiction for a hydrogen addiction, who do you think will make and control that "commodity"? There is no where on the planet where hydrogen can be found. Keep you from trying biofuel, ethanol, used cooking oil, the "industry" keeps it something you could not produce yourself. And keeps you under control.

If I was big oil this is exactly what I would want a 15 year multi-trillion dollar boondoggle, it is a nice cushion as they make over $100 Billion per year after taxes. This little story hits on all cylinders the realists, the scientists, the accountants, layman, environmentalists, but that's all it is, a good story and good PR, spin for all, but it will have no results at the end, just a lot of unfulfilled promises. And it keeps you distracted long enough so that not enough people ask the right question. Why wait for hydrogen ? why not use ELECTRIC? NOW, not in 15 years.

So lets talk about BioFuels, BioDiesel, Ethanol etc,
Rudolph Diesels invention, the Diesel engine originally ran on vegetable oil, that's right no petroleum involved. 100 years ago food processing huge consistent quantities of vegetable oil was fairly difficult. Today we bio engineer seedless tomatoes, oranges and fruit that will not be bruised by

large picking machines, imagine what could be done for fuels. So why can't we go back to the original concept?

We need to be careful when evaluating an alternative to no-fossil fuels. With hydrogen so far off and so many people beating the drums of Global Warming the pressure will be on to find an alternative to oil. American Agri-Business will be very motivated to help you with biodiesel, ethanol, and all kinds of additives and derivatives that can either substitute for or augment fossil fuels. But Agri-Business is only acting in their own self interest, there is nothing they would rather have than a captive audience just as the oil companies do. Now there is one country with a good news story for Ethanol. Argentina managed in 10 years to go from straight petroleum to 100% compliance of using Ethanol, the experts all said it could not be done, the auto makers dragged their feet. Argentina passed laws which said if you want to sell cars here they must be capable of using Ethanol or don't sell your cars here. My point is if a tiny 3rd world country can get 100% compliance on their Ethanol initiative then so can the United States. By the way Ford and GM sell cars in Argentina that run on Ethanol. But it is not an answer for America., but there is a glimmer of hope.

This is very, very important Ethanol. Corn, sugar, or wheat grass and bio-diesel fuels are NOT an alternative for America, because of the massive quantities required. We would need so much of these crops there would be no environmental savings. We use 3 Billion barrels of oil each day in America. If we were to make fuel from crops look at what that entails. Huge tracts of land probably the total land mass of 2 or 3 entire states, plus reserves. All these crops would need not only huge pieces of land but also water, fertilizer, insect repellant, and sun. A drought or Katrina-like event would devastate our entire economy because the crops are now the fuel for our automobiles. This scenario does not give us added national security; it actually handicaps us against a rainy or dry season which sooner or later will occur. After the crops are ready to harvest there is still much more to do, they now need to be harvested, using big farm machinery. Massive amounts of crops mean massive amount of machines and manpower neither are inexpensive. Farm equipment does not run on Ethanol, nor would it make sense to convert industrial machines and the trucking industry first. The first Ethanol vehicles would be consumer cars. The harvesting would be spread out across a few times a year when ever possible but what it comes down to is an amount of crops which are about twice the size of the state of Nevada have to be harvested. This will draw labor from the farm labor pool, which will drive up the price of farm labor and normal foods. Normal foods will now be in competition with "fuel foods" , this will also increase the cost of normal foods.

Assuming the grass or corn or whatever the crop is now harvested it needs to get put onto trucks and rail cars and get shipped to begin processing. All the truck still use fossil fuel. Now imagine a huge industrial complex where an acre of harvested crops gets boiled down, processed and refined and converted into a few barrels of fuel. Look at all the time and energy that is used to process the crops into fuel. This is a tremendous overhead, a few acres per person times 300 million of us, is a staggering amount of anything. When you take the amount of land needed, the volatility of crops, even watering this amount of crops is a great cost. When you in the harvesting, trucking and processing you will find that this is not a solution for 300 million people. Whereas this can be looked at in the form of a workable solution, it is not a viable alternative on a large scale. So the people who want to promote flex fuels may have good intentions and on the surface it sounds like a good idea, it is not. There are 6 Billion people on the Earth some of which do not have daily food or water, it would be ill-conceived to think that acres and acres of crops could be planted for each person to use for fuel. We could not do it for our own country let alone the rest of the world.

The forces behind the latest rise in food prices — China's economic boom, a growing biofuels industry and a weak U.S. dollar — are global and not letting up anytime soon. Grocery receipts are bulging because the raw ingredients, packaging and fuel that go into the price of foodstuffs cost more than they have in decades. It's possible to trace the jump in food costs to the commodities markets, where the price of agriculture products and energy have reached multi-decade highs this year. Crude oil, which helps dictate the price of gasoline and plastic packaging, hit an all-time peak in September 2007. Wheat prices also climbed to a record. The run-up in commodity prices has as much to do with short-term supply and demand in each market as with long-term shifts in who produces and consumes those products.

China is the juggernaut. Rapid growth there — and in Brazil, Russia, India and other developing nations — has led to massive demand for raw materials, including energy to run factories and cars, metals to build infrastructure and beans and grains to feed livestock and people. China will import almost 50 percent of the world's oilseeds within a decade, becoming the world's largest importer, according to estimates from the Organization for Economic Cooperation and Development. The world is using more of its food supply to make fuel. Corn in the U.S. and China is being converted to ethanol, a gasoline additive. Europe is using more wheat for ethanol and rapeseed for biodiesel, a cleaner burning fuel that is mixed with regular diesel. Brazil has bulked up its production of sugarcane to make ethanol. Demand for corn from the burgeoning ethanol industry in the U.S. helped drive corn prices to a peak earlier this year, setting in motion a domino effect of price increases through the food chain as livestock raisers, food makers and retailers tried to recover costs. Corn prices have come off their high due to expectations for a huge crop this year, but prices remain historically elevated because of inflation across the agriculture market. A bushel of corn that went for about $2 a couple of years ago costs about $3.50 today.

Here is another reason why trying to grown a few million acres of ethanol grass will be a challenge. With a raft of studies suggesting farmers will be hard-pressed to feed the extra 3 billion people swelling the world's ranks by the year 2050, Columbia University professor Dickson Despommier believes a new model of agriculture is vital to avoid an impending catastrophe. "The reason why we need vertical farming is that horizontal farming is failing," he said. If current practices don't change by mid-century, he point outs, an area bigger than Brazil would need to become farmland just to keep pace with the demand. Vertical farms, where staple crops could be grown in environmentally friendly skyscrapers, exist today only in futuristic designs an on optimistic Web sites. Despite concerns over sky-high costs, however, an environmental health expert in New York is convinced the world has the know-how to make the concept a reality — and the imperative to do so quickly.

And there is a man at Tata Motors Inc. making a $2,500 affordable "People's Car" to be introduced for the masses first in India, then Pakistan and China. Which he will be marketing to the masses of 3BC. (3 billion consumers) His goal is to put a car with economic reach for anyone who wants one.

DESTROYING AMERICA

Chapter 14 - The End of Oil   Leadership, Vision and the Future

But there is a silver lining.

Hydrogen is not a workable solution in the next 20 years. Biodiesel has promise but without some huge breakthrough in the amount required or a way to really concentrate the fuel it is not a feasible alternative, experts are concerned if there will be enough food to feed all the people of the earth in the coming decades. But there is a way to reach the end of oil, stop the pollution, lower carbon emission, slow global warming, and eliminate our dependence on foreign oil and increase our National Security, through the end of Oil. When I originally started reading on this topic I was overwhelmed by the amount of good, detailed, credible sources and research. Hydrogen seems like a clean burning no-brainer. But when you dig deeper you find out that it takes as much electricity as burning a full tank of gasoline to separate the hydrogen molecule out of water, so what is the point? You don't win you just use the same amount or a little less fossil fuel it becomes an endless cycle. When you look at the quantities needed to make biofuel viable it quickly becomes almost impossible. And it has bad side effects to the food economy. So what is the answer? The answer is renewable energy.

In 1974 after the major oil crises the US government commissioned a study from the CIA on the vulnerability of the oil production facilities, refineries, storage areas and pipelines in the Gulf region. It is a well know fact that that the finding showed that the refineries are soft targets in a highly combustible environment. Not much has changed in 30+ years. A simple pipeline disruption can have a disastrous impact on our entire economy. Our economy is so dependent on foreign oil that you could make a case that it is a matter of national security. Why after 30 years have we not finished implementing a plan B? The main reason is that the oil companies pay the politicians very well.

If this recent event is an indicator of something that is coming then our dependence on oil is a matter of national security and we should do everything possible to end the dependence. 172 AL Q Terrorists caught in Saudi Arabia (CNN) – "Saudi security forces have arrested scores of suspects in a terror plot involving attacks on senior officials and government oil, military and security installations, a Saudi intelligence official said Friday." But something CNN, FOX and other news sources are not telling you, why this is very significant, and why you should be concerned. Up to now UBL and Al Qaeda have been focused on the infidels, a Jihad, they have not attacked any fellow Muslims, nor in the Kingdom or Saudi Arabia.

So now if the rules have changed and they are willing to sacrifice their fellow Muslims, on the Kingdoms sovereign property, then all bets are off, "why should I care": here is why, there are only 3 places in the world where 8 million barrels of oil are pumped per day, not surprisingly all of them are in the Persian Gulf. The only thing standing in the way of $500 per barrel oil prices is the willingness of Al Qaeda to attack these strategic places and spill Muslim blood in the process. We are talking about an out in the open refinery not a hardened ICBM missile silo, by and large they are unprotected from military grade weapons. Panic and chaos will take over on the markets once any attack takes place, all they need to do is disrupt these high volume places near Abqaiq. Even an unsuccessful attack will cause panic and greed to shoot prices up. An "unsuccessful" attack can have devastating economic effects.

Second ALQ has stayed out of Saudi Arabia for more than one reason, let us just say if they were caught there are no limits on what the authorities there can do to you or your family but if they are now willing to target places within the kingdom anything is now fair game. And if somehow they do manage to overthrow the government with fanatical insiders in the UAE military UBL will inherit an arsenal of grade AAA US weapons, not old Russian crap. Even if they do not over throw the governments there are numerous soft targets which could wreak havoc in petroleum production. Moreover, ALQ does not have to a very "successful" attack, to succeed to triple the price of oil, the markets would take care of the rest, this would cause economic chaos throughout the world, and actually more economic damage than any weapon ALQ could get their hands on. If oil at $70 per barrel costs us $3 per gallon, $200 per barrel equates to $9 per gallon, the economic impact will have a ripple effect throughout every industry and will drive costs through the roof. They (ALQ) could even buy oil price options to make a killing when it happens. $200+ per barrel, will push up the prices on everything dependent on fuel, Postage, trucking, UPS, FedEx, Electricity, the CPI and Inflation indexes would go of the chart, etc, etc, etc. Lastly, picture a few insiders at a Saudi military installation. Forget a truck full of fertilizer, and an improvised 747 improvised-plane-suicide-missile, imagine them getting their hands on several F-16's and flying to Ghawar with a full compliment of real US missiles, and bombs. Oil is no longer an answer.
http://www.cnn.com/2007/WORLD/meast/04/27/saudi.arrests/index.html

Think Outside the Barrel

As I mentioned earlier Rudolph Diesel's invention, the Diesel engine originally ran on vegetable oil, imagine if diesel was synonymous with clean burning fuel instead of big dirty diesel engine. Our current growing consumption of 22 Million barrels per day can reduced by over 75% in 10 years if we set the goal and execute the plan. Not by sitting and dreaming about getting off oil but by making hard decisions and standing by them.

Not Nuclear, not biofuel, not hydrogen, we need renewable energy. Instead of living hand to mouth or paycheck to paycheck whichever cliché you prefer, the United States will invest in renewable resources. If a man is hungry you teach him how to fish, not make him a sandwich. This is like owning the house instead of renting it, we will have our own renewable resources which will provide adequate energy for our entire country. These renewable resources will be delivered on a reliable mature fully working energy grid. The US Government will purchase all electric utilities, this is how the energy will get to you, if the government owns it then we control the prices.

Rather than the power plants running on fossil fuels the US government will take on an Apollo like program. The US government will either by subsidize, incentive or direct expenditure start a national program for renewable energy on par with the linking the East coast and West coast by Railroad. Many US Energy experts say that parts of America are the "Saudi Arabia of wind", the Department of Energy has these studies, and they have done nothing with them. We will build wind farms where suitable, and where it makes the most sense. The Dutch did this very successfully in the 16th Century and the technology available today makes it all the more appealing. The wind farm in Palm Springs CA is a great real world example it produces power for over a million homes, the residents run their air conditioners 9 months a year there, it works it is real its not the Jetson's. The USA needs to invest in our infrastructure put in wind farms, to power our cities, not continue dumping money down the drain on fossil fuels.

America will also take advantage of the great weather that we have in our deserts, 365 days of annual sunshine will power photovoltaic cells and provide solar power to our country. Placing solar energy farms where there is a natural abundance of sunlight and a minimal of inhabitants is a great idea. Areas where no one has ever lived can now provide and endless stream of energy to our country. Think of all the full time solar power and even part time locations that there are in our country. Solar is expensive to build but very low maintenance, and the technology keeps getting better. Now we can harness the power of the sun, the most powerful energy source we know. Reinvest in our country to be free of dependence of any oil. People who have property in good energy production areas can start or join energy consortiums to give access to people who do not live in an energy production area; everyone can put energy into the system and get paid for it. If the government incents this behavior it will happen.

We will also have tidal energy farms, which harness the power of the waves, just like the famous power plant at Niagara Falls, and the Hoover Dam, and yet another source will be geothermal power, and we will have our own fossil fuels as a backup supply. Possibly even have some nuclear power plants just as a plan C. Our energy production will be diversified and highly renewable. Now with a steady supply of renewable energy from the sun and the tides and the wind on a mature and reliable power grid we can make a change for the better. You no longer need to consider hydrogen or Ethanol because now you can run your car on electricity. This solves numerous problems at once.

Your car can be powered just like your laptop. And I'm talking about a robust, stylish, responsive car not a golf cart, a car you would want to buy, except that it does not use gas.

This is NOT a golf cart 0 to 60 mph in 4.0 seconds, 165 mph top speed

This will also reduce demand and drive the price of oil down. It will free us from our dependence on a region of the world where we have no business being and have long overstayed our welcome, nothing positive has ever come out of the relationship in the Middle East. They are a drug dealer and we are the addict. You see today's real electric car, NOT hybrid, a hybrid is still chained to the gas pump, and goes no where without gas. But today's electric cars get over 300 miles per charge. The one from Tesla motors goes from 0 to 60 in 3.9 seconds with a top speed of 185 mph, this is not a golf cart, and it runs on NiMH laptop batteries, not even the better Lithium Ion ones. $5 a charge to go 300 miles.   http://www.teslamotors.com/ at $98,000 it competes with the Porsche, but they can make a consumer version. Or someone else will. Imagine if you could also write off 150% of the cost of your car if you were one of the first people to buy one, in a 24 month "jump start" program, with the write off amount reducing each year.

Ask: Why NOT ELECTRIC ?

Infrastructure is built and is mature, plug in your car at home

It is here now, and ready batteries get better and better

The US could put in wind farms and solar and have renewable energy for far less than the cost of the war in Iraq, which would last for 50 years and reduce Co2 and the power companies will buy all the electricity we can make, no fossil fuel no pollution everyone's happy, makes electric cheaper, and it is a long term solution instead of a band aid every month

Why are we waiting for hydrogen? Bio-diesel, Ethanol, Electricity is here NOW.

You can put a solar panel on your house and drive for free

For those that think GM tried this and it failed they did not, GM did not want a car model that it could not make revenue from servicing and maintaining. You see the EV1 had no oil changes and no tune ups. As a testimonial to this all 500 EV1 owners asked to buy their cars at the end of the lease and GM said NO. $1.7M dollars was offered by previous owners for the last 80 cars, giving GM $24,000 for a $16,000 vehicle, instead of taking the money GM turned it down and spent over $600 per car to have all these EV1 cars destroyed. Much more information on why this car was killed can be found on the links below. But you do not have to be a sheep, SUVs do not have to weigh 9000 pounds, cars do not need to get 20 mpg, and you do NOT have to run your car on gasoline, you just have NO alternatives. But you are NOT a slave, you just have not demanded anything intelligent from your elected officials, you need to get off your ass and ask for something intelligent from your elected officials.

Just as previous leaders had vision and invested in important infrastructure for our country, including the Interstate Highway act, and the rural electrification act, and the Great Railroad, this is a great undertaking for our generation. But this is the only government project ever embarked on with a positive return on investment. Only government has the kind of capital budget to make something like this work. Instead of $50 gas fill-ups imagine a $5 recharge for 300 miles, every dollar invested would pay itself back 100 times. Look at the impact here alone $25 for a month or car charges (subsidized) or $250 for gas. This is a tenfold savings and if the government can not give you healthcare but it can give you cheap electricity and you can take your $200 savings in gasoline and put it towards your own healthcare. And for the government there is no incremental expenditure, no hidden costs, we get off the cycle of fill up, empty tank, fill up again. And we buy the windmills and solar cells and other equipment from American companies, we invest in our future.

Once the energy production farms are in place this gives us the ability to transition off fossil fuels at our own pace. The government could incent people to expedite the pace. But in any event you could reduce oil consumption by 75% over 10 years and reduce imports to zero. Remember the first cell phones that were big as a brick and would have a dead battery before the end of the day and laptops that ran for 30 minutes, the first generation electric cars have all these experiences to build from so that these mistakes are not repeated. With the right government incentive this could be very painless conversion to the average person.

Assuming this wind/solar initiative and grid purchase costs us $1 Trillion dollars how do we pay for it? Well reducing our daily oil consumption (today's usage) by 11 Million barrels per day.

11 million barrels x 365 days x $70 per barrel = $275 Billion Dollars/year payback period is 4 years, if oil creeps up to $100 per barrel the amount is $400 billion dollars/year

The money saved on oil will obviously find its way back into the economy and will have a multiplier effect since it is coming from each individual consumer. I do not know that a formal payback is necessary; I mean what is the payback on an aircraft carrier? A deep space probe? A unused ICBM missile? Yucca Mountain? The Bridge to Nowhere?

These above items have no economic viability this renewable energy project frees us from fossil fuel, foreign oil, dirty money, wars in bad places and eliminates the #1 cause of pollution in our country. (what is that worth?)

Our Government has wasted more money that we will ever see, they always speak about our children's future they owe us this project to insure that we have a future.

The oil companies do not want you to consider this and the Government has known for over 15 years. As a matter of fact, if the oil companies were smart they could take some of their $360 Billion dollars in profits from last year and invest in building these wind farms and solar farms with no help or loans from anyone and pocket a huge piece of the pie. But they will not because they are busy buying diamond plated yachts.

Petroleum has enjoyed a 100 year monopoly because of non thinking, "abundance", pay-offs and the status quo. At a total of 22 Million barrels of oil per day (total current consumption fact) x $70 per barrel x 30 days = $46 Billion dollars per month spent (total) on oil. Oil recently touched a high of $100 per barrel and it may just be the start. For $46 Billion dollars per month there has got to be a better way! And there is. As we have found out since 9/11 a few cents out of every tank full of fuel that we buy falls into the wrong hands. That was a few cents per fill up at $30 per barrel of oil. Oil is now at $70 per barrel. It is one thing to not be aware that money was getting to the wrong people, but now that we do know it is unconscionable that we continue to fund our own deaths. Since our President was from Texas he chose to look the other way on this issue, and many others.
Demand over the next 20 years will continue to drive oil prices higher and higher with the industrialization and rapid growth of many "3rd" world countries. (In particular China) It is not in OPECs best interest to help with extra supply and there are many experts that agree that the Saudi Region can not keep a sustained higher output for long. It is certainly in our best interests of "National Security" to not be dependent on a bunch of guys who live in the 12th century. And our entire economy be tied to one product.

A large number of experts have calculated a way to use renewable energy and replace 40%-80% of our dependence on oil. The wind farms in the Palm Springs CA area produced enough electricity for over 500K homes, so this is not a far out "Jetsons"-futuristic kind of idea rather just one of leadership. Air conditioners run 8-9 months of the year in Palm Springs CA. We have regions in the US that can provide a very large amount of wind power for our country. Solar power is more expensive but the US is also known to have a few desert areas with 360 days of sunshine every year. If we covered just 7% of the surface of the State of Arizona with GE photovoltaic cells we would have enough energy to power all of America (GE web site). Remember the Dutch mastered this 400 years ago with no technology.

Breaking the Big Oil dependence: (facts)
We/The United States uses 20-24 Million barrels of oil per day. use 22 million bbl/day
Common Average is: 22 million/bbl/per day these are huge numbers,
50 to 60% of this daily usage is bought from imports.
So here is the basic math 22 Million bbl per day total,
11 M barrels per day is from imports,
to reduce the imports by 50% to 80% over the next 10 years.
Use WIND and SOLAR and TIDAL and Geothermal maybe a little Nuclear power instead of oil.
11 Million barrels x $70 per barrel x 30 days = $23.1 Billion dollars per month
This is $276 Billion dollars per year just for oil imports,
and $400 Billion per year if oil hits $100 per barrel.

The primary numbers for renewable energy (wind) estimate that for $200-400 billion dollars we can build adequate "wind farms" that can eliminate 40%-80% of our need for oil, I am aiming low but the math is incredible. Wouldn't it be worth spending $400 billion dollars to be free from oil? Yes. The electricity produced can also be used to create electricity for cars. Think of the health benefits alone. No more filling stations, plug in anywhere.

Billions of dollars saved as a % Reduction in current oil imports:
assumes oil at $70/barrel (at 11m bbl/day)

5% $13.8 Billion/yr

10% $27.6 B/yr

30% $82.8 B/yr

50% $138 B/yr   We reduce our imports by 6 million barrels per day here

75% $207 B/yr   We can almost eliminate oil imports at this point

This is straight math and being fairly conservative. Electricity works it is stable and we already use it. All we need to change is where the source of the energy comes from. Power plants can harness the energy from the wind and solar farms instead of burning fossil fuel as if it were the 1700's, this really is not that hard a concept. If we can reduce only our oil IMPORTS by 30% is not worth spending $200-500B dollars to save $100 Billion dollars per year every year??? We can eliminate importing oil. We need to act on the plans that the Department of Energy has that we paid for, they have been sitting around since 1991.

By reducing our oil consumption, this also adds 5m barrels of oil back into the world market (Total daily demand worldwide is 70m/bbl/day) this lowers the demand this will equate to lower prices (5-20%) reduction considering a 10% reduction in price per barrel that is another $2B/month saved, not to mention the health and environmental benefits from not using and burning 11m barrels of oil in our country. I don't think any of us would mind our electric bill cut in half or a car that does not pollute or a power plant not dumping tons of bad stuff into the environment each day. Clean renewable power, less pollution and greater national security.

This project pays for itself in 36-48-60 months and as a worst case scenario 10 years, no other government project is ever positive, ever. The government has known about this since at least 1991! They could have had the wind farms built and paid off already. We need to go after this like an Apollo program, $100-$200 Billion in subsidies; we give other industries (oil) 20 times that many incentives. They have put various alternative plans in the works since the 1973 oil embargo, but never act on any of them.

So where does the money come from? Hey the government (you and me) pick up the tab, and this is a bill I would be happy to pay. Here's why: this will be the ONLY Govt. project that will actually make money. The current Bill from the CBO for the Iraqi "Peace" is $2.4 Trillion Billion dollars as of November 2007, who knows what it will be when we are done. And if we had renewable energy a few years ago maybe the whole Middle East debacle would never have happened. For less than one-tenth the cost of the Iraqi-war every person, business and home in America would receive a real tangible monthly benefit. $500 Billion dollars to be free of these unstable countries and a century of pollution is a small price to pay; with a payback of over $100 Billion per year, you have to ask if we did this in 1991 where we could be today. We have the money to build tanks, explore Mars and go back to the moon lets have Bin Laden keep his fricking oil too. 6-8% of Germany's total electricity is currently generated from wind farms. But a Texan just does not have the balls for this. 80% of France's power is from Nuclear Energy.

My research is in the reference section but you are welcome and I encourage you to do your own. If you agree with me all I ask is for you to email your

Congressman and Senator and tell them that they can continue their multibillion dollar research on hydrogen but that:

You want renewable energy now, and electric cars now. If you disagree please tell me where I failed and line up for the $10 gal/gas. If you can remember back to the Clinton Administration you were getting Universal Healthcare its 12 years later do you have health care yet? You will get hydrogen on about the same schedule. Renewable Energy Now.

Electric NOW: .02c per mile, not a theory,

Today not 30 years away

Leadership, Vision and the Future

If a non scientist normal guy like me can figure a way off to get us off oil, decrease dependency on hostile nations, and reduce pollution imagine what a room of real experts can do! It is time to use all the technology that we have to get our country back, get the politicians engaged and working for us. Email them, call them, join Blogs, join Web communities and groups, and discuss the real issues. Tell them to stop squabbling over meaningless crap and programs which solve nothing and never will and to eliminate programs that never did anything other than create government jobs. Our problems in government really are fixable and it will not be easy, but not if none of our elected officials choose to do anything about them or worse continue to hide from the real problems. Let your representatives know what is on your mind and tell them what the real issues are. The longer our elected officials continue to hind behind the tent stakes of stupidity the worse the real problems will get and be even harder to solve. We are the generation that gets the check I am sorry to say, but the sooner we settle the charges the better off we will all be. . The sooner we table the real issues for an intelligent discussion the sooner a real solution will emerge. At one time there were no street lights in our country, and 95% of the citizens worked on farms. After World War 2 there was no highway system and the threat of nuclear war loomed over our heads everyday. Because of our American spirit, because of our intellect, because of our pride and heritage we have persevered and prospered and created a society that is the envy of the world.

In the 1960s with limited technology and many, many man hours of hard work we landed our first Apollo mission on the moon. President John F Kennedy commented on the Apollo program saying: "we do these not because they are easy, but because they are hard". Ronald Reagan challenged Mikhail Gorbachev to "tear down this wall" and free your citizens from the bonds of Communism. So you can see from these past examples just how far a little vision and leadership can go. Because we have been devoid of leadership and vision in our elected officials certainly does not mean that the American dream is not alive and well, quite the contrary it has been laying dormant waiting for a challenge. Waiting for the opportunity to take a dream and make it a reality. The time to lead by manipulation and fear has passed. The era for vision has arrived it is a new American Century and time once again to rise to greatness, time once again to astonish the world with American know how, ingenuity and creativity. This is our future and it is time to lead our country to greatness once again.

Recommended Reading:

American Theocracy: The Peril and Politics of Radical Religion, Oil, and Borrowed Money in the 21stCentury – Kevin Phillips (and other books by Kevin Phillips)

Freakonomics: A Rogue Economist Explores the Hidden Side of Everything – Steven D Levitt

Body of Secrets: Anatomy of the Ultra-Secret National Security Agency – James Bamford
also- A Pretext for War

Sleeping with the Devil: How Washington Sold Our Soul for Saudi Crude – Robert Baer (ex-CIA) also- See No Evil

Imperial Hubris: Why the West Is Losing the War on Terror – Michael Scheuer

Twilight in the Desert: The Coming Saudi Oil Shock and the World Economy – Matthew R Simmons

Ghost Wars: The Secret History of the CIA, Afghanistan, and Bin Laden, from the Soviet Invasion to September 10, 2001 – Steve Coll

Against All Enemies: Inside America's War on Terror – Richard Clarke

Contact the Author: www.destroying-america.com

Chapter References:

Chapter 2

http://www.safehaven.com/article-1942.htm

http://www.nchc.org/facts/cost.shtml Very Conservative source Healthcare
rose 7.9% overall in 2004

http://www.msnbc.msn.com/id/21309318/

htp://www.financialsense.com/stormwatch/2005/0624.html

http://moneycentral.msn.com/content/P146055.asp

http://www.mises.org/ Search CPI

http://www.shadowstats.com/cgi-bin/sgs/

http://www.businessweek.com/the_thread/economicsunbound/archives/2006
/08/real_wages_stil.html

Footnotes: and random ramblings

Here are some facts that should bring this point home
National Debt
So what your share of the national debt will be: Can you write the US Gov a check
for $440,000
David M. Walker, the nation's top accountant, is instead touring the country to warn
Americans about the consequences of a federal debt he says is on an unsustainable
course. "If [the candidates] don't make [the debt] one of their top three priorities, in
my opinion, they don't deserve to be president and we can't afford for them to be
president," he told CNN.
The federal debt has soared during the last two decades -- from $2.13 trillion in
1986 to $5.22 trillion in 1996 and $8.51 trillion in 2006.
<http://www.cnn.com/2007/US/03/28/federal.debt/index.html>
The federal debt now stands near $9 trillion. The way programs such as Social
Security, Medicaid and Medicare are structured, the government will incur an
additional debt of $50 trillion during the next 20 years, according to GAO figures.
The $50 trillion total amounts to about $440,000 per American household, Walker
said.
Government Math Part One: Here are few very interesting points of light
Government spending for Social Security and Medicare alone will increase from
about 7 percent of the U.S. economy to almost 13 percent by 2030, and to more than

15 percent by 2050, Bernake said. ****** Lets add 5% since the government is usually off by about 335% since health costs are rising 20-75% per year I would say they are way off.
http://news.yahoo.com/s/ap/20061004/ap_on_bi_ge/bernanke;_ylt=ArrrosmhHwG Wy48I9brE7peyBhIF;_
<http://www.publicdebt.treas.gov/opd/opdint.htm>, or about 18 cents of every one of your tax dollars. **** Please note payment of this debt is tied directly to the Federal funds rate, which has been at a 30 year artificial all time low brought on by the dotcom Tech bust of 2000 and 9/11 which is now being followed up by the mortgage meltdown. When the rate goes up the interest payment goes up so 18 cents becomes 20 cents or 25 cents (or much more). As you well know the national debt only grows, as will the payments. Isnt it funny that the only time you can use the word Trillion in a sentence is in government math or for rocket science?   If we connect the dots here…in a few years.....seems that almost 50% of every tax dollar will evaporate instantly, which means taxes will go ….? what not down?! ......read my lips......... <http://www.msnbc.msn.com/id/15064460/>

OK so the government sucks at this math thing how about the consumers? According to the NY Times, the number of people paying at least 30 percent of their gross income on housing increased significantly over the past five years. In New York City, at least 50 percent of people pay 30 percent of their income on housing. In Southern California, this balloons to 74 percent. The most surprising figures are found in Boulder, Colorado and College Station, Texas where more than 45 percent of people with mortgages spend at least 50 percent of their income just on housing. This means that if the average median income in the US is $45,000 or $3,750 per month,
spending 50 percent of your pre tax income on rent equals to a monthly payment of $1,875. For the same income level, taxes probably amount to $750 a month, which leaves an after tax income of $1,125. Assuming that miscellaneous expenses such as heating, home phone, cell phone, internet, and cable bills come to $300 a month, THIS LEAVES YOU ONLY $206 per week!
<http://biz.yahoo.com/fxcm/061003/1159894075369.html?.v=1>
In true discretionary income ($825 per month) which is an extremely small. This goes to show how stretched consumers are at the moment. The savings rate in the US is negative, which means that most people are dipping into their savings to fund their spending. Incomes are not growing at the same pace to help relieve some of that burden but what is most worrisome is the fact that low income counties have seen the biggest hit. These are the people who can least afford to shop aggressively this holiday season. ***** And they have dipped into savings for the last 17 months; put that $5 Latte down!
Well...yeah but at least we are healthy!   <http://www.cbpp.org/8-26-04health.htm>
Data that the Census Bureau released in 2004 show the number of people who lacked health insurance coverage throughout the year rose to 45.0 million. Think they can buy health insurance on $206 a week?
OK, Yeah but we got cell phones, dvd players, Ipods, blogs, digital cable, satellite

TV and were gettin' a shiny new $1.2 Billion dollar 1,500 mile fence put in at the border!
<http://www.cnn.com/2006/POLITICS/09/29/fence.congress.ap/index.html>
And we'll hang the entire health of the economy on Santa's sleigh.......what a great formula....

http://www.fxstreet.com/news/forex-news/article.aspx?StoryId=25d40c98-97bc-489e-b88d-659ca74aee6d But in order to measure " inflation "
"Overall prices, by a gauge of inflation tied to the consumer spending numbers, rose by 0.2 percent in August, after excluding energy and food." How do you not include 2 primary necessities of life when you are trying to calculate inflation of the necessities of life? I wonder what the inflation rate would be with some $3 per gallon gas thrown in there. Wouldn't inflation apply to the food you need to buy and the gas you need for your car? Who made up this government math? Well I guess it would be the government experts! ?
http://www.msnbc.msn.com/id/16922582/   US Savings lowest level in 73 years

The median U.S. household income is currently $43,200 and the typical family's credit card balance is now almost 5% of their annual income. The typical consumer has access to approximately $19,000 on all credit cards combined.
Based upon the two statistics above copied directly from the credit card facts web site one would have to ask the question since $43,200 is the median, which means half the people make less than that amount, why would you extend $19,000 credit, which is between 6 months to a full years income for these families. What is the criteria? Some kind of magic formula. More than half of all people with credit cards are using less than 30% of their total credit card limit. Just over 1 in 7 are using 80% or more of their credit card limit.
Approximately 14% of Americans use 50% or more of their available credit, and this group carries an average of 6.6 credit cards. 48% of consumers carry less than $5,000 of debt. This includes all credit cards, lines of credit, and loans-everything but mortgages. Nearly 37% carry more than $10,000 of non-mortgage-related debt as reported to the credit bureaus.

Chapter 3

http://news.bbc.co.uk/2/hi/americas/6920458.stm $20 B in arms to Saudis/10 yrs

Chapter 4

http://www.findarticles.com/p/articles/mi_m1571/is_6_15/ai_53913242

Total federal-government workforce just hit nearly 18 million, according to a new study by Paul C. Light of the Brookings Institution, reported in the January 1999 edition of Government Executive magazine.

http://govexec.com/features/0199/0199s1.htm

http://www.washingtonpost.com/wp-dyn/content/article/2006/10/05/AR2006100501782.html

Total US Workforce 140 Million, 2001; U.S. Bureau of Labor Statistics;

http://www.independent.org/publications/tir/article.asp?issueID=19&articleI

http://www.census.gov/govs/www/retiretechdoc.html

http://mwhodges.home.att.net/state_local.htm Great resource

http://mwhodges.home.att.net/florida/headcount.htm

US GDP almost 20-44% of spending, and another 13% for compliance/REG

http://mwhodges.home.att.net/mwhodges.htm Many great stats

http://www.cbo.gov/showdoc.cfm?index=3213&sequence=2 45M on SS

http://www.nchc.org/facts/cost.shtml Very Conservative source Healthcare rose 7.9% overall in 2004

http://www.policyalmanac.org/social_welfare/welfare.shtml 2.1M 5.1M children

http://www.cnn.com/ALLPOLITICS/stories/1999/03/29/welfare/ 2.9 M Minimum

http://www.washingtonpost.com/wp-dyn/articles/A49955-2004Sep25_2.html 2004 5M

http://money.cnn.com/magazines/fortune/global500/2006/performers/compa nies/biggest_employers/index.html Who are the largest employers, how many employees do they have?

Chapter 5

http://www.opensecrets.org/lobbyists/index.asp?showyear=2006&txti ndextype=s

http://www.cnn.com/2007/WORLD/asiapcf/05/28/china.health.reut/index.html

http://www.usatoday.com/money/industries/food/2007-05-29-china-drug-regulator_N.htm?csp=34

Chapter 6

http://www.ocrwm.doe.gov/ym_repository/index.shtml   Yucca Mountain

http://www.reviewjournal.com/lvrj_home/2007/Jan-23-Tue-2007/news/12133717.html

http://www.state.nv.us/nucwaste/yucca/loux05.htm

http://www.heritage.org/Research/Budget/wm889.cfm   Bridge to Nowhere

http://www.csmonitor.com/2004/0615/p02s01-uspo.html

http://www.solari.com/learn/articles_missingmoney.htm   Missing Money

http://www.ft.com/cms/s/f0eff690-fc0a-11da-b1a1-0000779e2340.html
How can $2,700bn disappear? Financial Times UK The global financial system seems to have a black hole

http://www.heritage.org/Research/Budget/wm1048.cfm   Railroad to nowhere

http://www.heritage.org/Research/Budget/bg1840.cfm

http://www.heritage.org/research/features/budgetchartbook/charts_S/s5.cfm

http://www.heritage.org/research/features/budgetchartbook/charts_S/s5.cfm

http://news.yahoo.com/s/ap/20070215/ap_on_go_ot/iraq_reconstruction_waylt=Av26QlOpIPMkOk0s1CB_peYDW7oF   Billions Squandered in Iraq

http://www.findarticles.com/p/articles/mi_m1571/is_41_16/ai_72328754
HUD missing 59B

http://iraqforsale.org/facts.php Halliburton Waste

http://news.yahoo.com/s/nm/20070404/bs_nm/jacksonhewitt_fraud_dc

http://www.post-gazette.com/pg/07103/777689-84.stm

http://www.msnbc.msn.com/id/17509045/

http://www.cbsnews.com/stories/2007/02/16/ap/politics/mainD8NAKC0O5.shtml

Great debt link   http://home.att.net/~mwhodges/debt_a.htm#culprit

Chapter 7

http://www.prisonpolicy.org/factsheets.html#Prison_and_The_Economy

http://www.impactlab.com/modules.php?name=News&new_topic=318http://www.aef.com/industry/news/data/2001/1855 You need drugs

http://www.medialifemagazine.com/news2001/aug01/aug13/1_mon/news2monday.html LIST over $4.5 B 2001

http://www.newstarget.com/010315.htmlhttp://content.healthaffairs.org/cgi/reprint/20/2/100.pdf master plan laid out in 2000 for "aggressive growth"

http://money.cnn.com/2005/06/28/news/fortune500/adage_report/index.htm

http://adage.com/images/random/LNA2006.pdf $8.5 B in 2005 tied for 4th

Car, Retail, Telecom, Pharma(fin/banking)

http://psychrights.org/Drugs/AllenJonesTMAPJanuary20.pdf

http://www.ablechild.org/declaration%20of%20refusal.aspx

http://www.wildestcolts.org/

http://www.mercurynews.com/mld/mercurynews/news/breaking_news/15887999.htm

http://people.ucsc.edu/~rstone/issue.htmlhttp://www.mercurynews.com/mld/mercurynews/news/local/states/california/northern_california/15207211.htm

Detail $4B spent in CA in the last 5 years, $600M for one, and $1.2B for

9000 beds, etc, …

http://www.adpsr.org/prisons/costs.htm

http://news.yahoo.com/s/ap/20070221/ap_on_re_us/california_prisons;_ylt=
AoGTwPyyma.1eViBkZ.cSeVvzwcF

Chapter 9

http://www.amazon.com/Education-Myths-Special-Interest-Believe-
Schools/dp/0742549771

http://www.edreform.com/index.cfm?fuseAction=section&pSectionID=59
Researcher Greene debunks several purported myths at the heart of assumptions
about efforts to reform troubled public schools. He begins with the conventional
wisdom that increased spending on schools leads to improved education. Citing
national statistics on school spending, Greene asserts that most arguments about
inadequate spending are based on anecdotes not facts. He concludes that even if
schools in poor urban areas were provided with more funds, there is no guarantee
they would use the funds effectively. Other myths that he debunks: social problems
such as poverty contribute to low academic performance, smaller class sizes
produce improvements, certified teachers are more effective, teachers are underpaid,
public schools' performance has declined, private schools are more racially
segregated than public schools. These myths are perpetuated by powerful interest
groups, including teachers' unions, asserts Greene. Whatever readers may think of
Greene's research, he provides an interesting perspective to the ongoing debates
about what ails public schools and how to improve them.   If ever an institution
needed input from someone working outside the standard paradigm, public
education is it. To many people, it is obvious the system is not working well, yet
suggestions from anyone who is not part of the system are automatically dismissed.
Jay Greene is an established and well-respected researcher of education issues,
whose only agenda is to elevate the quality of public and professional debate about
education. This book addresses a basic problem facing those who wish to improve

our schools: many assumptions about education have never been tested in a scientific manner, and many have no basis in fact. Often these untested assumptions form the rationale for expensive programs that consume much time and money with little result. In some cases, blind acceptance by the public of untrue "facts" prevents consideration of novel approaches. Greene has analyzed the research related to several crucial issues and pointed out that while some of it is worth considering, much of it is of little or no value. This book suggests a fresh framework for inquiry into the problems that plague our schools and frustrate everyone who wishes to see good education available for all children.

Thanks and References

http://freestateproject.org/org/faq

http://citizensforreasonableandfairtaxes.blogspot.com/

http://www.schoolandstate.org/

http://www.kevinpchavous.com/index.htm

Steven David Horwich – Why Education Stinks and What can be Done about it

Bill Allin – Turning it around: Causes and cures for today's social problems

Kevin James Bondelli – Evaluation of the Effectiveness of the Traditional Education System

Chapter 9

http://www.scrapthecode.com/facts.htm

http://www.salestax.org/library/skousen_16history.html

http://www.opinionjournal.com/extra/?id=110007139

http://www.thelawthatneverwas.com/new/home.asp

http://www.apfn.net/Doc-100_bankruptcy20.htm

http://www.wealth4freedom.com/16thHistory.htm   http://givemeliberty.org/

http://www.mises.org Search: Income tax

http://www.ustreas.gov/education/fact-sheets/taxes/ustax.shtml

http://www.tax.org/Museum/1901-1932.htm

http://www.msnbc.msn.com/id/17454852/   Stick it to Joe Taxpayer

http://news.yahoo.com/s/nm/20070109/bs_nm/usa_economy_taxes_dc

http://www.usatoday.com/money/industries/telecom/2005-06-30-taxes-usat_x.htm

Chapter 10

http://www.deathpenaltyinfo.org/FactSheet.pdf

http://www.msnbc.msn.com/id/11472172/page/2/

http://www.nrlc.org/abortion/facts/abortionstats.html

Chapter 11

http://www.cdc.gov/nccdphp/dnpa/obesity/trend/maps/

Chapter 12

1. $11 Billion to $22 billion is spent on welfare to illegal Aliens

http://www.fairus.org/site/PageServer?pagename=iic_immigrationissuecenters7fd8

2. $2.2 Billion dollars a year is spent on food assistance Programs such as food stamps, WIC, and free school lunches for illegal Aliens.

http://www.cis.org/articles/2004/fiscalexec.html

3. $2.5 Billion dollars a year is spent on Medicaid for illegal Aliens.

Http://www.cis.org/articles/2004/fiscalexec.HTML

4. $12 Billion dollars a year is spent on primary and secondary School education for children here illegally and they cannot speak a word of English!

http://transcripts.cnn.com/TRANSCRIPTS/0604/01/ldt.0.html

5. $17 Billion dollars a year is spent for education for the American-born children of illegal aliens, known as anchor babies.

Http://transcripts.CNN.com/TRANSCRIPTS/0604/01/ldt.01.HTML

6. $3 Million Dollars a DAY is spent to incarcerate illegal Aliens.

Http://transcripts.CNN.com/TRANSCRIPTS/0604/01/ldt.01.HTML

7. 30% percent of all Federal Prison inmates are illegal aliens. (this is correct but the data is skewed because border crossing is a federal offense)

Http://transcripts.CNN.com/TRANSCRIPTS/0604/01/ldt.01.HTML

8. $90 Billion Dollars a year is spent on illegal aliens for Welfare & social services by the American taxpayers.

Http://premium.CNN.com/TRANSCIPTS/0610/29/ldt.01HTML

9. $200 Billion Dollars a year in suppressed American wages are Caused by the illegal aliens. (possibly)

Http://transcripts.CNN.com/TRANSCRIPTS/0604/01/ldt.01.HTML

10. The illegal aliens in the United States have a crime rate that's two and a half times that of white non-illegal aliens. In particular, Their children, are going to make a huge additional crime problem in the US

Http://transcripts.CNN.com/TRANSCRIPTS/0606/12/ldt.01.HTML

11. During the year of 2005 there were 4 to 10 MILLION illegal Aliens that crossed our Southern Border also, as many as 19,500 illegal Aliens from Terrorist Countries. Millions of pounds of drugs, cocaine, meth, Heroine and marijuana, crossed into the U. S from the Southern border. Homeland Security
http://www.house.gov/mccaul/pdf/Investigaions-Border-Report.pdf

12. The National Policy Institute, "estimated that the total Cost of mass deportation would be between $206 and $230 billion or an Average cost of between $41 and $46 billion annually over a five year Period."
http://www.nationalpolicyinstitute.org/pdf/deportation.pdf

13. In 2006 illegal aliens sent home $45 BILLION in remittances Back to their countries of origin. http://www.rense.com/general75/niht.htm

14. "The Dark Side of Illegal Immigration: Nearly One Million Sex Crimes

Committed by Illegal Immigrants In The United States ".
http://www.drdsk.com/articleshtml

Chapter 13

http://www.forbes.com/home/free_forbes/2007/0416/070.html

http://www.msnbc.msn.com/id/21195621/

http://www.msnbc.msn.com/id/21154137/

Chapter 14

www.nrel.gov/wind/wind_potential.html

http://www.ronsaari.com/stockImages/windmills/WindFarmPalmSpringsCA.php

http://www.osti.gov/energycitations/product.biblio.jsp?osti_id=6282249

More at www.doe.org but you have to click around.

GE has great information on their site as well: www.ge.com

GE is ready for the future

http://www.mnforsustain.org/energy_truth_about_hydrogen_wilson.htm

http://www.news.cornell.edu/releases/Dec02/Alt-energy.hrs.html

http://www.popularmechanics.com/technology/industry/4199381.html

http://peakoil.blogspot.com/2006/10/truth-about-hydrogen-popular-mechanics.html

http://www.gepower.com/businesses/ge_wind_energy/en/index.htm

http://acore.org/blog/?p=15

http://www.ev1.org/msg/11.htm

Additional References:

www.destroying-america.com

http://chondorsrantsoftheweek.blogspot.com/

http://www.nrel.gov/

Our own arm of the government focused on renewable energy

Weak US Dollar   http://www.msnbc.msn.com/id/21018869/

Who holds treasury notes   http://www.msnbc.msn.com/id/17424874/

http://www.treasurydirect.gov/NP/BPDLogin?application=np

Corporate take over of govt http://www.msnbc.msn.com/id/17346255/

Unskilled Immigrant labor http://www.msnbc.msn.com/id/19101228/

National Debt out of control http://www.msnbc.msn.com/id/15064460/

One Day Boycott http://www.msnbc.msn.com/id/18492185/

Falling Dollar   http://www.msnbc.msn.com/id/18383804/

National Debt Danger http://www.msnbc.msn.com/id/17050732/

Wealth Gap http://www.msnbc.msn.com/id/16115342/

Downsize DC http://www.downsizedc.net/

http://www.nationmaster.com/graph/ene_oil_con_tho_bar_dai-oil-consumption-thousand-barrels-daily&int=-1   OIL Consumption 20,000 BBL per day

http://www.scribd.com/doc/193920/Whats-wrong-with-American-Education Education

http://www.associatedcontent.com/article/249455/what_is_wrong_with_american_education.html?page=2   Education

http://www.cdc.gov/nccdphp/dnpa/obesity/trend/index.htm   Obesity

http://obesity1.tempdomainname.com/subs/fastfacts/obesity_what2.shtml   Obesity

http://www.washingtonpost.com/wp-dyn/content/article/2007/10/15/AR2007101501359.html?hpid=topnews   Social Security

http://citizensforreasonableandfairtaxes.blogspot.com/search/label/Education%20Myths   General

http://nces.ed.gov/fastfacts/display.asp?id=372   Education Stats http://www.schoolmatters.com/ Education stats and financials

http://www.ncjrs.gov/txtfiles/165476.txt Gun Owner NON NRA data 1994

http://www.gunowners.org/fs0404.htm   Gun Numbers (Pro gun but good data)

Creditcard info http://www.creditcards.com/statistics/credit-card-industry-facts-and-personal-debt-statistics.php

http://www.cnn.com/2007/LIVING/wayoflife/10/19/stretch.paychecks.ap/index.html Poor are getting poorer, WalMart adjusting numbers based on paycheck date to paycheck date variance.

http://www.justice.gov/dea/demand/speakout/05so.htm Social costs vs. drug costs

http://www.pbs.org/wgbh/pages/frontline/shows/drugs/special/math.html Drug$

http://www.crime-research.org/analytics/759/ 1995 $57B in the US alone

http://news.yahoo.com/s/nm/women_dc;_ylt=Aiorph9C.p3wXO5SmCWpFyADW7

http://www.nrlc.org/abortion/facts/abortionstats.html

http://www.msnbc.msn.com/id/21195621/ Raw Material price increases

http://www.washingtonpost.com/wp-dyn/content/article/2007/10/15/AR2007101501359.html?hpid=topnews   Boomers

http://news.yahoo.com/s/ap/20071029/ap_on_re_us/dropout_factories High Schools are Dropout Factories
http://www.msnbc.msn.com/id/21154137/ Vertical Farming

http://www.cnn.com/2007/TECH/science/09/18/driving.iceland/index.html   Iceland NO fossil fuels

http://www.dhs.gov/xnews/releases/press_release_0520.shtm

http://www.ci.yuma.az.us/az_dept_commerce.pdf

http://mediamatters.org/items/200704110003?offset=20&show=1

http://www.signonsandiego.com/news/mexico/tijuana/20070815-9999-1m15bparrest.html

http://72.14.253.104/search?q=cache:Y-UCj8ngqFYJ:www.ccis-ucsd.org/news/SDUT-4-16-06.pdf+yuma+AZ+border+crossing+arrests&hl=en&ct=clnk&cd=3&gl=us

http://www.mexidata.info/id1434.html

http://www.hispanicvista.com/HVC/Opinion/Guest_Columns/121806Nguest.htm

http://www.latimes.com/news/nationworld/nation/la-na-fence25aug25,1,1555869.story

http://www.foxnews.com/story/0,2933,195791,00.html

http://www.kvia.com/global/story.asp?s=7260896 Fence Opposed by Texas land owners

http://www.msnbc.msn.com/id/21195621 Consumer Price Increases

http://www.desertinvasion.us/data/invasion_numbers.html

http://citizensforreasonableandfairtaxes.blogspot.com/

http://www.econlib.org/

http://www.cagw.org/site/PageServer Citizens Against Government Waste

http://www.heritage.org/

http://www.just6dollars.org/ Americans for Campaign Reform

http://www.kevinpchavous.com/index.htm Education Reform

http://www.globalissues.org/Geopolitics/ArmsTrade/

http://www.ge.com/products_services/energy.html

http://ge.ecomagination.com/site/index.html#wind GE Wind

http://www.gepower.com/home/index.htm

www.ingramcontent.com/pod-product-compliance
Lightning Source LLC
Chambersburg PA
CBHW031503270326
41930CB00006B/229